THE INTERNATIONAL CIVIL SERVICE

The International Civil Service
A Study of Bureaucracy: International Organizations

HANS MOURITZEN

Dartmouth
Aldershot • Brookfield USA • Hong Kong • Singapore • Sydney

© H. Mouritzen 1990

All rights reserved. No part of this publication may be reproduced, stored in a retrieval system, or transmitted in any form or by any means, electronic, mechanical, photocopying, recording, or otherwise without the prior permission of Dartmouth Publishing Company Limited.

Published by
Dartmouth Publishing Company Limited
Gower House
Croft Road
Aldershot
Hants GU11 3HR
England

Dartmouth Publishing Company
Old Post Road
Brookfield
Vermont 05036
USA

British Library Cataloguing in Publication Data
Mouritzen, Hans *1952–*
 The international civil service : a study of bureaucracy : international organizations.
 1. International organizations. Administration
 I. Title
 354.1

Library of Congress Cataloging-in-Publication Data
Mouritzen, Hans.
 The international civil service : a study of bureaucracy : international organizations / Hans Mouritzen.
   p. cm.
 Includes bibliographical references and index.
 ISBN 1–85521–163–7 : $44.00 (est.)
 1. International officials and employees. 2. International agencies. 3. Bureaucracy. I. Title.
 JX1995.M73 1990
 354.1'1—dc20   90–41725
                                                              CIP

ISBN 1 85521 163 7

Printed in Great Britain by
Billing & Sons Ltd, Worcester

Contents

List of Figures ix
List of Abbreviations xi
Preface xiii

INTRODUCTION 1

PART I: THE ENVIRONMENT, THE VALUES AND THE ROLES OF THE INTERNATIONAL CIVIL SERVICE 9

THE ENVIRONMENT VS. THE INTERNAL LIFE OF THE INTERNATIONAL CIVIL SERVICE 9

CRUCIAL ACTORS IN THE ENVIRONMENT OF THE INTERNATIONAL CIVIL SERVICE 10

THE VALUES AND GOALS OF THE INTERNATIONAL CIVIL SERVICE 12

THE ROLES OF THE INTERNATIONAL CIVIL SERVICE 14
   The Bridge-Building Roles 14
      Conflict Preventor 14
      Passive versus Active Mediator 15
      Communication Facilitator 17

Further Political Roles	17
Boundary Guardian	17
Instrument for Powerful IO Member (-Group)	18
The Substantial Roles	19
IO Identity Supporter	19
Initiator	20
Operator/Controller/Observer	20
Expert/Coordinator	21
IO Representative *vis à vis* Non-Members	21
How Much Influence is Exerted?	22
THE ENVIRONMENT REVISITED: THE CLIENT/ AUTHORITY CONSTELLATION AND ITS IMPLICATIONS FOR THE INTERNATIONAL CIVIL SERVICE'S POLITICAL VALUES	22
THE NEED FOR BRIDGE-BUILDING: VARIOUS TYPES OF IO	24
The Need for NATO International Civil Service Bridge-Building	27
PART II: HOW INTERNATIONAL IS THE INTERNATIONAL CIVIL SERVICE?	35
THE PROBLEM OF INTERNATIONALISM FOR THE INTERNATIONAL CIVIL SERVICE: THE NATURE OF THE PROBLEM	35
IS IT A CRUCIAL PROBLEM?	37
COULD AND SHOULD SOMETHING BE DONE ABOUT THE PROBLEM?	38
THE RELEVANT PROPOSITIONS	41
The Principle of Merit versus Quota	41
NATO: Merit versus Quota	43
The Existence of a Career Service	44
NATO: Career Service?	45
The National Career Value of an ICS employment	46
The National Career Value of a NATO IS employment	46
Leadership	48
NATO: Leadership	49
Bureaucratic Ideology	50
NATO: Bureaucratic Ideology	51
Reachability: Generally and in NATO	52

THE NATO INTERNATIONAL STAFF INTERNATIONALISM 53

CONCLUSION: HOW CAN ICS INTERNATIONALISM BE
   IMPROVED, AND WHAT HAS NATO DONE? 54

SHOULD NATO HAVE DONE DIFFERENTLY? 55

COULD NATO HAVE DONE DIFFERENTLY? 59

UNCERTAINTY AVOIDANCE 60

PART III: THE INFLUENCE OF THE INTERNATIONAL CIVIL SERVICE: WHERE, HOW AND WHY? 67

INTRODUCTION 67

HYPOTHESES ON THE INFLUENCE OF THE INTERNATIONAL
   CIVIL SERVICE 67

THE ISSUE-AREA MODEL 68
   The 'Height of Politics' and ICS Influence 72
   The Needs' Location and ICS Influence 76
   Conclusion 77

THE SELECTION OF NATO ISSUE-AREAS FOR
   INVESTIGATION 78
FORCE PLANNING 79
   The Decision-Making Process in General Terms 80
   The Roles and Influence of the IS in the Process 82
   Explaining the IS Influence in Force Planning 86

INFRASTRUCTURE · 89
   The Decision-Making Process in General Terms 90
   The Roles and Influence of the IS in the Process 92
     Ceiling 92
     Cost Sharing 93
     Programming of a Slice 94
     Exemption from ICB 95
     Inspections 96
     An Installation's Residual Value 97
     Conclusion: The Roles and Influence of the IS in the Process 98
   Explaining the IS Influence in Infrastructure 99

INFORMATION	105
NATIS' Own Activities	106
Member-countries' Information Activities	107
The Secretary–General's Identity Role	110
The Roles and Influence of the IS in Information	112
Explaining the IS Influence in the Information Area	113
PART IV: CONCLUSIONS, METHODOLOGY, AND METHOD	123
CONCLUSIONS	123
The Issue-Area Model	125
Lessons for the Model?	127
The ICS Preparation of Meetings, etc.	127
The Secretary-General's Contribution to Information	128
The Two Fundamental Properties	128
Should Stipulations be Revised?	129
METHODOLOGY AND PERSPECTIVES	130
Suggestions for Further Research	132
APPENDIX ON METHOD	133
BIBLIOGRAPHY	137
INDEX	145

List of Figures

INTRODUCTION

1 NATO's institutional structure 7

PART I

2 The main conceivable ICS roles, and the values they are believed to serve 13

PART II

3 A model of factors determining ICS internationalism (self-control) and the implications of these factors for ICS influence capability 39
4 The formal structure of the NATO IS 49

PART III

5 The four basic characters of issue areas 70
6 The basic character of an issue area determining the ICS influence in the area 71

7 Basic character of issue area determining the ICS influence in the area 78
8 Committees under the North Atlantic Council 79
9 NATO infrastructure programming cycle 91
10 Nominal and real values of annual NATO infrastructure expenditures 100
11 The number of A-grades in IS Directorates, and the long-term trend for three selected Directorates 102

List of Abbreviations

ASG   Assistant Secretary General
CDI   Conventional Defence Improvement Effort
CONIO   Conference of National Information Officers
CS   Civil Servant
DPC   Defence Planning Committee
DRC   Defence Review Committee
DPQ   Defence Planning Questionnaire
DUI   Danish Institute of International Affairs
EC   European Community
EEC   European Economic Community
EPC   European Political Cooperation
FAO   Food and Agricultural Organization
GATT   General Agreement on Tariffs and Trade
HQ   Headquarter
i   interview
IAEA   International Atomic Energy Agency
IC   Infrastructure Committee
ICAO   International Civil Aviation Organization
ICB   International Competitive Bidding
ICS   International Civil Service
IGO   International Governmental Organization
ILO   International Labor Organization
IMCO   Intergovernmental Maritime Consultative Organization
IMS   International Military Staff

INGO	International Non-Governmental Organization
IO	International Organization
IPPC	Infrastructure Payments and Progress Committee
IS	International Staff (NATO)
MC	Military Committee
MNC	Major NATO Commands
MODIO	Ministries of Defence Information Officers
MSC	Major Subordinate Commands
NAA	North Atlantic Assembly
NATIS	NATO Information Service
NATO	North Atlantic Treaty Organization
NPG	Nuclear Planning Group
OAS	Organization of American States
OECD	Organization for Economic Cooperation and Development
OEEC	Organization for European Economic Cooperation
SACEUR	Supreme Allied Commander Europe
SEATO	South East Asia Treaty Organization
SG	Secretary-General
SHAPE	Supreme Headquarters Allied Powers Europe
SNU	Danish Government's Committee on Security and Disarmament
SSF	Danish Social Science Research Council
UKMF	United Kingdom Mobile Force
UN	United Nations
UNCTAD	United Nations Conference on Trade and Development
UNEF	United Nations Emergency Force
UNESCO	United Nations Educational, Scientific, and Cultural Organization
UNHCR	Office of the United Nations High Commissioner for Refugees
UPU	Universal Postal Union
US	United States of America
WEU	Western European Union
WHO	World Health Organization
WMO	World Meteorological Organization

Preface

As admittedly overstated by one of my interviewees for this book, himself an international civil servant:

> ...to understand the daily life of an international civil service, consider the troubles of a national civil service, multiply by the number of member countries, and square it. [The latter operation referring to the civil/military dichotomy in NATO] (interview 6)

Even though not agreeing fully with the above statement, this book argues that there *are* fundamental peculiarities of an international civil service compared with a national one, making it worthy of independent consideration and theory. This book lays the foundation for theorizing on the international civil service (that is, the bureaucracy of an international organization), including its interplay with the delegations of national governments in the so-called 'multilateral diplomacy'. Even though focusing on the international civil service, one can learn, in this process, a great deal about the nature of governments, including their almost paranoid fear of losing their grip on the allegedly 'international' civil service.

With the current trend in world politics, however, allowing for an increased freedom of manoeuvre for international organizations, there is all the more reason to try to improve the creativity of their civil services, not least in view of the criticism that has been raised against some UN agencies for malfunctioning or even outright incompetence. In this book, suggestions for reform that should make 'international' civil services more truly international and innovative than is the case today, are derived from a theoretical model.

One of the main theses of the book is that the influence of international civil servants (including the Secretary-General) relative to that of their national colleagues, varies not so much between international organizations like the UN, the EC and NATO, but rather between issue areas within one and the same organization. Hence, a general 'issue-area model' is constructed that can account for the roles and influence of international civil servants in various areas. It is challenged empirically in three areas of NATO activity.

The book's audience should not only be university students and scholars in political science and administration, but hopefully also international civil servants themselves, and national civil servants, who plan for a career as international civil servants, or who expect to be stationed in their government's delegation at an international organization.

A total of 43 interviews were carried out, most of them at NATO in Brussels, both in the (civilian) International Staff and in four national delegations (see the Appendix on Method). For obvious reasons of anonymity, no mention can be made of interviewees, but all are thanked for their interest and generous allotment of discussion time. I should express my gratitude to information officer, John Høst Schmidt, NATO Information Service, for invaluable practical assistance in connection with my visits.

The main source of economic support for the project that resulted in the present book has been the SSF, but support has also been granted from NATO, SNU and DUI. Last not least, I should like to emphasize the Danish Army Academy (Hærens Officersskole) for flexibility in connection with my leave of absence to carry out the present study.

I thank my present colleagues and students at the Institute of Political Studies, University of Copenhagen, for interesting discussions, and also dr.phil. Henrik S.Nissen at the Institute for Contemporary History, University of Copenhagen, and my wife, Trine Dam Kofoed, herself a civil servant. I alone carry responsibility for the contents of the book, including the errors and misinterpretations that may remain. My mother, Mrs G. Mouritzen, has typed large parts of the final manuscript in a completely satisfactory way. Finally, I thank my family for their patience and endurance.

Hans Mouritzen
Copenhagen
February, 1990

Introduction

An international organization is a treaty-bound, multilateral body, whose members are of different nationality.[1] International organizations have, like states, their own bureaucracies and civil servants.[2] By 'international civil servants' are here understood civil servants employed by and paid by an international organization (IO, see below).[3] Their work varies, of course, between IOs and between issue-areas within one IO. But typical services amount to the preparation of meetings between IO member-countries' representatives at various levels, the chairing of meetings, and the writing of meeting reports. In some cases, they also play a role in the implementation of IO decisions. In carrying out these services, the international civil servant (CS) plays the roles as expert and coordinator, which, under favourable conditions, can make the CS[4] an initiator in relation to member countries' representatives. It will also be natural for the CS to try to prevent member-country conflicts or mediate in such conflicts, once they have arisen. One of the reasons for this is that the CS represents the IO as such. As expressed by Claude (Claude, 1964, p. 174; cited from James, 1971, p. 54):

> In a very significant sense, the identity of every organization... is lodged in its professional staff. Members, stockholders, or citizens may control the organization, but they cannot be it; the staff is the organization.

This identity role is also crucial in itself, particularly as we are dealing with such relatively weak actors in the international system as IOs, who need all the identity they can get. Their permanent staff of civil servants, including their

Head, the Secretary-General, is precisely what makes IOs distinct from ongoing international conferences.

Many of the services of international civil servants mentioned above can be recognized from their colleagues in a national setting. What, then, distinguishes the two phenomena, a national and an international civil service (ICS)?[5] Is the latter, in the first place, a phenomenon in its own right, worthy of independent consideration? One obvious difference springs from the heterogeneity of staff. The civil servants of an international bureaucracy are recruited from the member countries (their bureaucracies, typically) of the IO in question. This implies a highly heterogeneous staff as to, for example, language, culture and working routines, making daily work more troublesome and complicated. There is, undoubtedly, a difference as to heterogeneity between a national and an international civil service, generally speaking. This, however, is hardly the essential difference between the two phenomena. After all, certain national administrations also live with civil servants of different religious or ethnic backgrounds. What constitutes the ICS as a phenomenon in its own right is its position in the international system. Its special characteristic is that the actors beneath it, that is, the IO members, are, by far, the most powerful actors in the world, that is, nation states. For these, there is a great deal of prestige in filling as many ICS posts as possible with their 'own' people, and being able to control or influence them subsequently. The problem, hence, for the ICS is the following: will it be possible for the individual civil servant to uphold loyalty to the IO that the CS is employed by and paid by, or will the CS rather be encircled by the native country (its bureaucracy), and so be under stronger influence from here than from the employer? In other words: how international can the 'international' civil servant be expected to be? The problem, subsequently, will be referred to as the problem of internationalism or self-control for the ICS[6] (or the 'dependency problem' for the individual civil servant vis-à-vis the CS's home country). The problem of self-control exists in all allegedly hierarchical systems, if one is to believe modern organization theory; the point here is only that it is significantly exacerbated in a milieu consisting of the world's most powerful actors. These powerful actors have, of course, powerful civil services. Apart from trying to influence their own fellow countrymen, the national civil servants also survey the ICS activities in more general terms. In the absence of parliamentary control or significant press control of the ICS,[7] the national civil services may, by virtue of their sheer sizes relative to the ICS, be able to exercise a type of control that is *different* from, though no less constraining than, the types of control that national civil services themselves are exposed to.

A further characteristic feature of the ICS is the modest, and in some cases negligible, role that it tends to play in the implementation of decisions, compared with a national civil service. It is often left to member countries to implement a common decision in the IO; the ICS may then survey this implementation. It will seldom have any enforcement power, if it is dissatisfied with the national implementation; only in the case of the EC are there legal sanctions that may aid compliance with IO decisions. This peculiarity of the ICS springs from the same underlying cause as the preceding ones: the fact that we have weak IOs with strong members, given the nature of the present international system.[8] These members prefer to carry out as much of the implementation of IO decisions by themselves, in order to secure their own influence over outcomes. This peculiarity, though, is less fundamental than the one pertaining to self-control: there do exist, as we shall see, ICSs with full implementation responsibility, and a whole range of hybrids down to the situation where the ICS may only survey the various national implementations.

Finally, the ICS authority is not, as the authority for a national civil service, a reasonably coherent unit (a cabinet, a minister). It consists of representatives of allegedly 'sovereign' actors, with naturally divergent interests. It will be argued in this book that ICSs will design for themselves (or be allotted) significant bridge-building roles between these interests. It seems, on the average, that whereas the ICSs have less significant implementation roles than national civil services, they compensate by having more important bridge-building roles.

In view of these, more or less fundamental, peculiarities of the ICS compared with a national service,[9] one can legitimately wonder why the literature on it is so scant and poor as it actually is,[10] both in absolute terms and even more when compared with the voluminous literature on national or local administration.

> One significant indicator of the analytical vacuum that surrounds international bureaucracies can be found by looking at James March, *Handbook of Organizations* (... 1965). Nowhere in the 1247 pages of this 'bible' on organizational behavior and bureaucratic problems is there mention of an administrative structure for... international secretariats. Weiss (1975, p. xxii, note 12).[11]

Rather than being a sideline for organization theorists, the study of the ICS has been a sideline for – a few – international relations scholars[12] and for former international civil servants, drawing on their specific experiences (for example, Ranshofen-Wertheimer, 1945; Loveday, 1956; Stikker, 1966; van Wagenen, 1971; Hoggart, 1978; Lord Carrington, 1988). These latter studies can often be of significant idiographic interest, but they are seldom formulated systematically and in general terms, so as to facilitate comparison, not to speak of theory building.[13]

This 'state of the art' is even more paradoxical, when considering the rapidly growing number of IOs (both governmental and non-governmental ones), especially since World War II (for example, Bennett, 1988, p. 5). Their actual significance in the international system is, from an aggregate point of view, a more controversial matter (for example, among academic schools of 'international relations'). Few, however, would deny that even though nation states are, by far, the most crucial actors in world politics, there is a trend in current years in the direction of stronger IOs. One need only mention here the strengthening of the EC from about 1986 (for example, the European Single Act) and the improved opportunities for the United Nations (UN), presently, in the light of the existing *détente* between the superpowers in 1990. With strengthened IOs, their civil services should also be more attractive subjects for study than previously. A further argument in this direction is the criticism for lack of effectiveness or outright incompetence that has been levelled against ICSs (notably the UN and specialized agencies like UNESCO and UNCTAD) from many quarters (not least the USA and Great Britain).[14] Much of such criticism is probably politically motivated, but even a sympathetic observer (Weiss, 1986, p. 105) has stated that:

> The deterioration in the overall morale, competence, and objectivity of international secretariats is nefarious and worsening at all levels.

In order to evaluate criticism, and recommend possible 'cures' for ICSs, it is necessary to study them with more systematic, nomothetic ambitions than has been usual so far.

This book, inspired by the few systematic studies that, after all, exist on the ICS, will establish the foundation for general theory pertaining to the conditions, influence and creativity of the ICS and its civil servants. This foundation, with its general models and propositions, could serve as a framework for future studies – studies that could remedy the lack of literature on the ICS and improve the 'state of the art'.

Part I focuses on the salient environment of the ICS, in wholly general terms. What are the main types of actors in this environment, and what are their relation to the service? What are the values, goals and roles of the ICS, imposed by external actors or self-designed? Will this tend to vary with the kind of IO with which we are dealing?

Having seen in Part I that member governments of the IO are the most crucial environmental actors for the ICS, we proceed in Part II to focus on the problem of internationalism, a problem that these governments are responsible for by holding a – more or less – tight grip on their fellow countrymen in the ICS. It is argued that this problem to a certain extent inhibits the ICS from delivering the services that these same member governments wish to get from the ICS, because it reduces the autonomy, initiative, and thereby also influence capability of the ICS *vis-à-vis* clients and member countries. It is also argued that the problem is self-reinforcing.

The fundamental conditions responsible for the problem of internationalism cannot be manipulated. However, there are factors that *can be*, to the benefit of shaping more influential ICSs. We discuss some schools of thought on this question. A general model of determinants for the internationalism of the ICS is established. Furthermore, it is discussed why nation states, or their Foreign Services, to be more specific, may not even *want* influential ICSs.

Part III analyses where, how and why the ICS actually has an influence of its own. A general model of determinants for ICS influence, relative to that of national civil servants, is established. It lays the foundation for a theory of issue areas, in the sense that it asserts that the most essential factor determining the ICS relative influence is the 'basic character' of the issue area (see below). From the model follows that the influence of the civil servants, relative to their national colleagues, will vary strongly between areas with different 'basic character' – even though covered by one and the same IO. This corresponds with Michelmann's observations of the EC Commission's different levels of influence in different issue-areas (Michelmann, 1978, pp. 13, 231).

In accordance with the model, our unit of analysis is the individual issue area, not the IO. Three issue areas are selected as challenges for the model that each represents one of the three relevant basic characters for an area: a high politics area, where inter-state needs are fulfilled (NATO force planning); a low politics area, with inter-state needs (NATO infrastructure); and finally a low politics area, where intra-state needs are at stake (NATO information). As appears, the areas have been selected from the activities of one particular IO. There are crucial, both analytical and practical, advantages in this. Regarding the former, it allows us to presuppose that a range of environmental variables are constant (for example, the types of member countries, the IO's decision rules, and so on); hence, they do not disturb the effects of the relevant variables. On the practical side, there are certain obvious advantages as to research economy by the fact that the collection of empirical material can be concentrated to one IO (see also Michelmann, 1978, p. 3).

NATO embraces issue areas, which represent the three relevant types of basic characters – a necessary condition in the present context. Another reason for concentrating on this IO is that the literature on IOs and ICSs only to a very modest extent deals with NATO or other political–military IOs (see for example the classical work edited by Cox and Jacobson, 1974, or Bennett, 1988). The quite extensive literature on NATO and 'Atlantic Relations' (for example Sloan, 1986) concentrates on the policies of member countries and their mutual relations. Very little attention is dedicated to NATO's own institutional design. The literature on this latter phenomenon is to a large extent constituted by NATO's own publications, which, even though useful, avoid controversial issues and are written in a legalist and descriptive style. One of the reasons for this lack of literature is probably the secrecy traditionally surrounding security policy, which also inhibits empirical investigations of military organizations and alliances.[15] Another reason is mentioned by Jönsson (1986, p. 44):

> A common contention in the [international organization] literature, furthermore, is that international secretariats are not allowed to play a significant role in issue-areas which touch upon 'high politics' and involve – directly or indirectly – state security.

It is dubious, however, if this assumption is valid in the case of NATO. Already from an *a priori* viewpoint, it is obvious that

> ...NATO combines the traditional functions of an alliance with the institutions, procedures, and operations of an international organization.
> (Buteux,1983, pp. 4–5)

and

> ...NATO stands as much in the growing tradition of functional international organization as in that of military alliances. In NATO the two are intertwined to an unprecedented extent. (Jordon, 1967, p. VII; also Beer, 1971, p. 170)

The mere existence of a huge organizational apparatus, however, does not *prove* that it has significant influence *vis-à-vis* its environment (for example, James, 1976, p. 72). It can be a pure epiphenomenon, without a causal power of its own, without significant feedback on the actors that have created it.[16] But this is an empirical question that will be answered in Part III. The mere *existence* of a huge administrative organization makes it reasonable to try to remedy the lack of literature mentioned above.

The question of *temporal* delimitation of our empirical focus is, strange as it may sound, largely irrelevant to our reasonings, due to the fact that almost all the categories turn out to be constant, by and large, for the whole of NATO's history. As expressed by Harari and Bouza (1986, p. 41), inspired by a UN context:

> ...the puzzling phenomenon is not so much innovation but its frequent absence in international institutional settings.

The variation that is necessary for our present theoretical purposes is not diachronic, but synchronic, that is, between issue areas. Most of the illustrations, though, stem from the 1980s, as the interviewees' experiences are typically from this period. This decade has implied more challenges to the NATO civil servants than previously, as regards conflict prevention between member countries and mediation between them, as we shall see below (p. 27).

NATO's Institutional Structure

We should, first of all, briefly describe NATO's institutional structure (Figure 1), with special emphasis on the position of NATO s civilian administration in this structure. The administration's civil servants fulfil the defining characteristics stipulated for international civil servants: they are employed by the IO, and they get their salary from its budget.

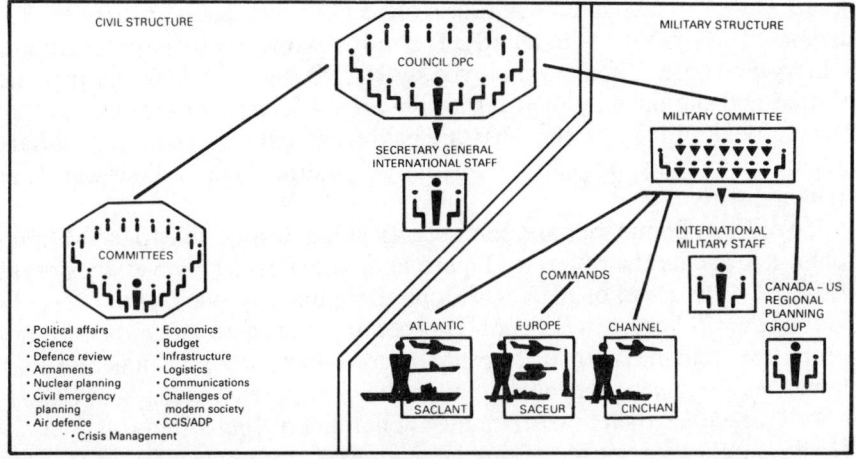

Figure 1 Nato's institutional structure
Source: NATO, *Facts and Figures*, 1984, p. 89

The civilian administration – in Figure 1, labelled 'International Staff' (IS) – is headed by NATO's Secretary-General. Its main tasks are to prepare and – on several occasions – to chair NATO meetings at all levels (and to implement a few types of decisions). At the top level, the Secretary-General is chairman of the North-Atlantic Council ('Council' in Figure 1). Member-countries are represented in this Council by their Ministers of Foreign Affairs at the semi-annual meetings; at the – approximately – weekly meetings in between, the countries' so-called 'Permanent Representatives' (Ambassadors) at NATO Headquarters (HQ) replace them. The ambassadors head their country's respective delegation of national civil servants – like the IS located at the NATO HQ in Brussels.

The North-Atlantic Council has set up a long range of committees (see the list of subjects for these committees in the left part of Figure 1). These consist of national civil servants representing their countries (typically from the delegation in question – in certain cases sent from their capital), together with a secretary and, normally, a chairman from the IS, analogous to the functioning of the Secretary-General at the top level.

The Military Committee (to the right in Figure 1) is a somewhat peculiar committee, consisting – apart from its chairman – of member countries' Chiefs-of-Staff or their permanent representatives (each heading a military section of their country's delegation at NATO HQ). The International Military Staff (see Figure 1) provides administrative support for the Military Committee, almost analogous to the IS in relation to the rest of the committees, and is like the IS, located at NATO HQ. It is, in terms of personnel, somewhat smaller than the IS (in 1989 about 250 military officers compared with around 325 academics –'A-grades' – in the IS). The military officers in the International Military Staff are formally employed by NATO, but in actual fact they are selected and stationed by their respective armed forces (services), as part of their national military career. They are paid from home (the national military budget) ; and hence they do not qualify as 'international civil servants', as stipulated here.

The military commands are, formally speaking, responsible to the Military Committee and its chairman (see Figure 1). In actual fact, however, the post as SACEUR – the Head of SHAPE (Mons, Belgium) and the Commander-in-Chief of the US Forces in Europe – is superior to the chairman of the Military Committee, both internally in the organization and *vis-à-vis* the outside world. The reason for this is probably that he shall not represent the national Chiefs-of-Staff (or, rather, their lowest common denominator), but instead his own and SHAPE's military expertise. There are national delegations in Mons (though much smaller than the Brussels delegations); but what counts is that SACEUR is not obliged to consult with national representatives, before making a statement.

SHAPE's staff amounted in 1987 to approximately 2400 military officers (excluding the approximately 200 officers in the national military delegations). It is largely staffed according to the same principles as the IMS (that is, national stationing, promotion and salary); again, therefore, its officers fall outside our concept of 'international civil servants'. In spite of this, however, we cannot avoid an analysis of the roles of the military authorities (in particular SHAPE) in the NATO decision-making process.

As already mentioned, the issue-area model will be challenged in Part III by observations from NATO issue areas and the influence of IS civil servants in these areas. Part II concludes with some recommendations for the reform of the NATO IS that should improve its creativity and influence capability.

Part I The Environment, the Values and the Roles of the International Civil Service

The Environment versus the Internal Life of the International Civil Service

> The major causes of growth, decline, and other large-scale changes in... [organizations] are exogenous factors in their environment, rather than any purely internal developments.   (Downs, 1967, p. 263; and also chapter II)

This is almost a truism; it is from its environment that demands, support and hindrances for the activities of an organization emanate. The following comparison is, however, obviously non-truistic: the environment is *more* crucial to the functioning and influence of an ICS than for a national civil service. This is one of Michelmann's conclusions on the basis of his investigation of a range of EC General Directorates (in the EC Commission) and their respective issue areas. Michelmann (1978, p. 232) sees the Directorates' autonomy, a category pertaining to their environmental relationships, [17] as the – by far – strongest determining factor for their effective functioning:

> It follows, of course, that other variables are of secondary significance for organizational effectiveness in the commission. Adequate performance with respect to internal variables is necessary for effectiveness, but it is not sufficient, and in the absence of autonomy one may conclude that it is largely irrelevant. Leadership, which is crucial to the functioning of most organizations, can have little impact on effectiveness in the absence of autonomy... the villains of the piece are national governments, unwilling to allow the commission the autonomy to become effective in those areas where it has clearly played no meaningful role.

From this, Michelmann (1978, p. 232) draws an important conclusion as to the applicability of organization theory in the study of ICSs:

> It would appear, therefore, that the analysis and reform of management practices (that is, reform with respect to the internal correlates of effectiveness) have a greater justification in a national administration than they have in the Commission, because chances for an impact on effectiveness are much greater in the former.

If this is accepted,[18] it explains neatly the tendency (mentioned in the Introduction) for the study of ICSs to be a sideline for international relations researchers rather than for organization theorists – in other words, the cleavage between students of national and international administration.[19]

Crucial Actors in the Environment of the International Civil Service

The following crucial actors in the ICS environment should now be stipulated. The authority for the ICS will typically be the supreme Council of the IO in question, consisting of representatives of the IO members. In the case of IGOs (International Governmental Organizations) that we are dealing with in this book, members are national governments, whereas in INGOs (International Non-Governmental Organizations, that is, transnational actors), members are private associations. Apart from being the employer, the authority pays the salary of the civil servants, and normally also the rest of the ICS budget (the latter, though, not by definition). The authority consists of '*authority actors*', that is, individual governments (IO members). The authority *eo ipso*, though formally speaking a unit, is seldom in actual fact a coherent actor in its own right. Moreover, disharmony between authority actors may actually be the order of the day. 'Authority', though, is often a convenient short-hand term.

The *clients* of the ICS are actors who are supposed to benefit from conscious and voluntary interactions with it. Clients that are simultaneously authority for the ICS (for example, if the authority has designed the ICS as a secretariat that should provide a service for its own meetings only) will be the most salient kind that one can logically imagine. Such '*primary clients*' not only formulate and pay for the services of the ICS, they are also in an optimal position to observe the quality of these services (see p. 23). They will probably get the very best treatment that the ICS can provide. The rest of the clients, here labelled '*secondary clients*', are typically situated in the 'backyard' of the IO member governments, that is, under their formal jurisdiction. Obviously, the closer they are situated to government circles and, hence, to an authority actor, the better their opportunities for complaint on bad service, and the better service will probably be provided by the ICS.

Identification actors are actors who sympathize with the official purposes of the IO in question, and who can support its civil service by virtue of pressure on their respective governments (for example, Harari and Bouza, 1986, p. 47). Furthermore, they can make an information/propaganda effort in the population or within key groups in the backyard of the member government. This could also affect the government in a positive direction, from the standpoint of the IO in question.[20]

Counter-groups are actors opposed to the IO's official purposes and crucial policies. They may include political parties (though hardly parties in government, of course). Analogous to the identification actors, they are relevant to the ICS either through direct pressure on government or indirectly by virtue of an information/propaganda effort in other directions.

Secondary clients, as well as identification actors, seek to promote their interests through direct contacts with the ICS. On a par with counter-groups, they may cooperate transnationally (even to create INGOs) in order to strengthen their positions. As examples could be mentioned the national agricultural organizations, associated transnationally and lobbying in the EC Commission in Brussels (secondary clients), the liaison between national UN associations (identification actors), and most of the European peace movements in the 1980s, cooperating across borders (counter-groups to NATO).

If we focus on one particular Directorate within an ICS, then obviously other Directorates in the ICS will be more or less crucial environmental actors. Some of them may be *competitors*, that is, rivalling for the same tasks and, hence, resources. As expressed by Downs (1967):

> There is an incessant jockeying for position in policy space by means of jurisdictional disputes as each... [organization] struggles to defend or extend the existing borders of its various territorial zones. (Downs, 1967, p. 276, and also Chapter XVII)

We shall return to 'boundary maintenance' and 'task expansion' below (pp. 14 and 17–18). Suffice to say here that there will be plenty of grey zones to struggle for between directorates with related official purposes. An ICS, or a Directorate within it, may also have competitors within other IOs, with roughly the same official purposes (for example, EPC and WEU can be seen as potential competitors to NATO, rivalling for tasks in the grey zones between them; or UNCTAD to GATT, both preoccupied with the structure of world trade, for example, Cox, 1969a, pp. 28–9).

The authority actors are, as described above, crucial to the ICS. What makes them even more crucial is that they have, at their disposal, large bureaucracies at stake, including civil servants covering the same fields as those of the IO/ICS. These *national civil services* are also, in themselves, salient actors for the ICS, interacting with it at all conceivable levels. In particular if they have permanent delegations attached to the IO/ICS Headquarters, they can observe and try to control the ICS activities in all phases of the decision-making process.[21]

The Values and Goals of the International Civil Service

As international civil servants were stipulated initially (p. 1), ICSs are different from mere aggregates of nationally stationed civil servants. The criterion regarding salary was made in order to single out employments that are purely formal. It is believed, with Downs (1967, p. 28) that:

> Every man's self-interest leads him to be most responsive to those who decide whether he shall retain his primary position and income.

We hence regard ICSs as coherent and stable organizations in their own right, with a reasonable degree of self-control.[22] They have at least a *potential* for being actors. It would be unfruitful, *a priori*, to rule out this empirical possibility. Hence, we shall regard ICSs as actors, albeit weak ones, of course, until manifestly proven wrong in each case.

Any actor can be ascribed two sets of ultimate values: its substantial (issue-specific) values and its political (issue-neutral) values (see for example Mouritzen, 1988, pp. 42–43). In Figure 2, this is done for ICSs. The substantial values of the ICS embrace the official purposes of its IO, be it the promotion of health, agriculture or security. They have been decided by the ICS authority. The political values include the ICS's own survival, together with its autonomy and influence capability. The latter refers to its ability to influence other actors, whereas 'autonomy' means its ability to resist the influence of other actors (see above).[23] Influence, in turn, means the modification of one actor's behaviour by that of another (for example, Cox and Jacobson, 1974, p. 3).

Autonomy and influence capability are, of course, empirically related. Saying that the ICSs are weak actors, as has been done casually so far, is another way of saying that they have low autonomy, that is, from their authority/primary clients, and also low influence capability. Still, there is no logical impediment to an ICS that has managed to acquire a certain autonomy from its authority (to some extent avoid its steering attempts), but has acquired no significant ability to modify the behaviour of clients or authority. There is, besides, no reason to believe that ICSs will not try to *improve*, like organizations in general, their modest status in these two regards, even though it is seldom more than marginally realistic, given the general primacy of nation states in the international system.

A goal (intermediate value, see Figure 2) of the ICS that I see as instrumental in relation to the three political values is relative harmony between the members of the IO, that is, the individual authority actors. Disharmony and conflict can be assumed to weaken the IO and perhaps even endanger its very existence in the long run. Such a development will, of course, also represent a threat to its ICS's survival. In any case, it will tend to reduce its influence capability: it will be harder for the ICS to modify the IO members' behaviour in the direction of the IO substantial values. Also, ICS autonomy will be

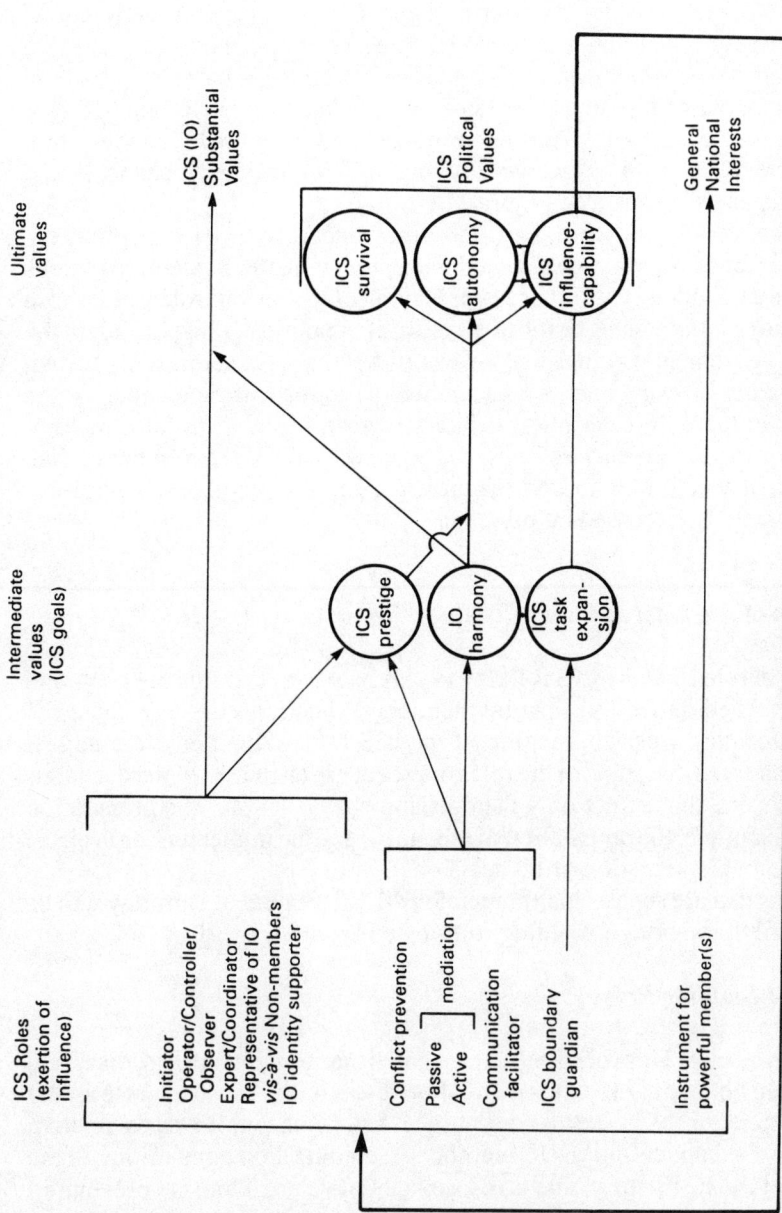

Figure 2 The main conceivable ICS roles, and the values they are believed to serve

For explanation, see text

negatively affected: the IO members' mutual suspicions will tend to be transferred to the ICS (is it, in fact, a 'Trojan horse' for a contending member or group of members?). This will make them less inclined to allow the ICS a little autonomy.

Apart from these three effects, the factor of IO harmony will also affect the ICS political values through a fourth channel. More harmony between IO members will probably lead to more IO integration and, hence, tasks to be solved in common. The lower degree of mutual suspicion will perhaps allow the ICS an increased role in the implementation of tasks. This IO and ICS task expansion will give the ICS further resources and personnel (growth!) and, hence, increase its influence capability, due to more influence channels and prestige in general terms (see Figure 2).[24]

A number of ICS activities, here subsumed under 'roles' (for a definition, see below) can be seen as instrumental in relation to the ICS goals and values (see Figure 2). Evidently, the successful playing of the various roles, be it those aimed at substantial values or those aimed at ICS political values, renders the ICS prestige (reputation) that will be useful for the safeguarding of its own political values. Prestige, hence, is seen here as an intermediate value for the ICS. Among the political values, influence capability will, in turn, make it possible for the ICS to play its roles, that is, exert influence, even better than before and, hence, further improve its prestige. This conceivable self-reinforcing mechanism is discussed on pp. 22–3.

The Roles of the International Civil Service[25]

A number of roles that the ICS is likely to play as *means* towards the goals and values stipulated above can now be mentioned. The roles are aggregates of activity indicating a certain relation of the ICS to its salient environment. It should be stressed that some of the roles may occur in all phases of the decision-making process, that is, not only the decision phase, but also the preparation phase (for example, the preparation of meetings) and the implementation phase (that is, the implementation of IO decisions).

The roles that are seen as instrumental *vis-à-vis* the goal of harmony will be described first: the bridge-building roles (see Figure 2).

The Bridge-Building Roles

Conflict preventor This role aims to prevent disharmony (conflicts, disagreements), even before it arises. It is difficult to distinguish it from the role as 'IO identity supporter' (see below) because a crucial means towards relative harmony is to convince various IO members, including their populations, of the blessings of the IO identity, that is, its substantial values. Conflict prevention also encompasses, though, the agitation in favour of specific IO policies or, negatively, against views that may threaten the IO consensus. The most fundamental effort towards conflict prevention is directed towards the IO member populations at large. In particular, the ICS may seek to encourage the identification actors to an extra effort, and to refute the arguments of countergroups.

Proceeding a step closer to governments, the ICS may seek to influence certain political parties in the 'correct' direction; perhaps, even attempts to interfere in party politics may be made (Cox, 1973, p. 175). Such interference will normally violate the IO's rules ('member-states' sovereignty', for example), but it can, of course, be done in a discreet fashion.

By the kind of systematic activity described here in the backyard of IO members, the ICS hopes to prevent governments being pushed into IO conflicts for domestic political reasons; quite to the contrary, they might be pushed in the 'correct' direction, from the viewpoint of IO consensus.

An example of ICS interference in domestic politics could be the playing on domestic French politics by the first ILO Director-General Albert Thomas (*ibid.*, p. 172). What gave Thomas a special leverage *vis-à-vis* the French Government, apart from his allegedly dynamic personality, was his own political platform in the French Opposition. Hence, it is possibly a somewhat special case.

Passive versus active mediator   Once a preventive effort has failed, and a conflict or disagreement has become manifest (not necessarily to the public though), a mediation attempt between the IO members will be a possibility.[26] 'Passive mediation' implies that a compromise is suggested to the contending parties, close to a weighted average of their initial positions. The advantage of this cautious type of mediation is obviously that it does not endanger the mediator's non-partisan image – something that could worsen conflicts rather than solving them.

'Active mediation' is mediation combined with initiation (see below). The ICS proposes its own independent ideas for the solution of conflicts/disagreements, ideas that are *not* designed as weighted averages of the parties' initial position. Instead, the ideas can be based on the ICS's conception of the IO's 'objective' common interests (but need not be so, by definition). As should appear, being an active mediator requires a stronger imagination, expertise (the reference to 'objective' common interests), or authority in broader terms, than passive mediation.

ICS active mediation could be illustrated by the establishment of the UNEF force in Egypt, as part of the solution to the Suez crisis (see Rovine, 1970, pp. 283–295). Even though the original impetus and idea was Canadian, the Head of the UN ICS, Secretary-General Hammarskjöld

...was able to outline its functions, structure, processes and location in a manner satisfactory to each of the contending parties and again, was able to do it quickly. He was the focal point for the process of international bargaining that went on throughout the period of crisis and was able to press particular positions and formulations not altogether pleasing to any of the parties, but without at any time losing their confidence. (ibid., p. 294)

The proposal and its implementation made it possible for the British and the French to withdraw militarily from the area, without losing too much face (giving them, *post hoc*, a reason for their military presence that sounded legitimate – protection of the Canal zone). In the delicate situation that existed, none of the Great Powers could really suggest the eventual solution, without causing others to oppose it; however, when proposed by the UN, with its authority and impartial image, none of the Great Powers found reason to oppose it. We have, hence, a situation, where (Cox, 1973, p. 160)

...major powers are known to be prepared to accept a course of action though unable or disinclined themselves to advocate it.

Such a situation may be overcome by ICS passive or active mediation.[27]

Whereas active mediation requires a certain prior authority on the part of the mediator, it will also, if successful, *further* enhance this authority (prestige) and, hence, influence capability of the ICS (see Figure 2). This actually happened in the case at hand: the prestige of the UN ICS and in particular its Head, the Secretary-General, was significantly increased (see Rovine, 1970, pp. 294–295). But if the ICS overplays its hand, that is, overestimates its own authority among the contending parties, then its active mediation will easily fail, and it may bring itself into disrepute with one or more of the parties (as happened later with the UN Secretary-General in relation to the Soviet Union). This, in turn, will lower its future influence capability and probably also its autonomy *vis-à-vis* member governments' control. In other words, active mediation is more of a chance game than passive mediation for the ICS, entailing both greater opportunities and greater risks for the ICS.

The mediation attempts of Joseph Avenol, the Secretary-General of the League of Nations (1933–1940), could illustrate passive mediation (Rovine, 1970, p. 419):

...his choice was limited to support of the Covenant [that is, the League Charter] at the expense of the Axis powers, or a compromise with Fascism and militarism at the expense of the League. Avenol chose the latter...

Even though passive mediation is probably much more widespread than active mediation, this rather 'extreme' example should illustrate the very essence of passive mediation: Avenol sought a (roughly) middle position between the contending parties in world politics, whereby he abandoned the principles of the Covenant or other conceivable bastions that he could have clung to (though probably in vain, it should be added).

It should be stressed, finally, that passive and active mediation can occur in all three phases of the decision-making process. The UNEF example pertained mostly to the implementation phase, as we saw. We shall now turn to the role as communication facilitator that can also be played in all three phases of the process.

Communication facilitator The communication facilitator brings together the contending parties and/or passes information between them (Young, 1967, pp. 62–64, 69–72; Rovine, 1970, pp. 441–442), for the purpose of bridge-building. By virtue of the ICS/IO's physical facilities, frequently with attached national delegations, that is, its central position in the IO member network (Jönsson, 1986, pp 40, 42, 45), the ICS will possess excellent opportunities to be communication facilitator. This role implies, of course, a more modest attempt towards bridge-building than do the two mediator roles. But it is probably a more widespread role for the ICSs to play. As examples could be mentioned the role of the UN General Secretary U Thant during the Cuban missile crisis of 1962 and his early service during the Vietnam conflict as a kind of limited substitute for direct diplomatic dealings between the United States and North Vietnam (Young, *ibid.*).

Further Political Roles

Boundary Guardian

As expressed by Downs (1967 p. 264),

> All organizations have inherent tendencies to expand.

These tendencies have already been touched upon above (see pp. 11, 14). Expanding, or at least maintaining, its boundaries is a means of securing an organization's growth (size), both in terms of personnel and in terms of resources in broader terms (task expansion or maintenance). The desirability of this, in turn, is explained by Downs (*ibid.*):

> The expansion of any organization normally provides its leaders with increased power, income, and prestige; hence, they encourage its growth.
>
> Growth tends to reduce internal conflicts in an organization.

There is no reason to believe that these tendencies (and their supposed reasons) should not also be widespread in ICSs, at least to some extent (Cox, 1969a, pp. 25–29; Cox and Jacobson, 1974, p. 7; McLaren, 1980b, p. 145). Unlike the ICS roles directed towards the substantial values, and to some extent the bridge-building roles, the role as boundary guardian is likely to be wholly self-designed.

It is always difficult to decide, whether overt task expansions can be ascribed to conscious ICS boundary maintenance, or to exogenous factors (or both). As a hypothetical example of boundary maintenance could be mentioned the declaration from NATO Secretary-General Manfred Wörner of 1989, condemning the Bulgarian suppression of citizens of Turkish origin (*NATO Review 1989/4*, p. 3). Even though not an entirely new field for NATO, one might regard the emphasis on human rights as a striving for task expansion, given the present East–West climate, where a sole reliance on the core tasks of the Alliance would seem a fragile basis for continued organizational growth.

Instrument for powerful IO member (-group)   IOs (and, hence, ICSs) have been described as 'depositories of legitimacy' (James, 1976, pp. 85–87; see also Rovine, 1970, pp. 445–447). This means that individual IO members can borrow some legitimacy for various measures, when described as part of an IO programme, or in the name of the IO in question. The more controversial the measures (for example, Great Power military invasions), the more eagerly this kind of borrowed legitimacy will be needed and strived for.

The instrument role, however, designates a more narrow phenomenon. The ICS is used here as a tool to serve the general policies of a powerful IO member (member-group), be it through instruction, anticipated reaction, or identification. The ICS autonomy, hence, is zero or negligible. This kind of relationship will, of course, be criticized by other members of the IO. But it is often difficult to verify in practice (even more, of course, for the outside researcher). For instance, it should be distinguished from a sheer community of attitudes between a member actor and the ICS, with no instrumentality involved. The verification is also made difficult by the fact that instrumentality will hardly be expressed in rhetoric, as it violates crucial norms for an ICS (see Part II, p. 36).[28]

UNCTAD's ICS is a loyal supporter of the G77 (the group of developing countries) in the North–South dialogue, also in rhetoric. As expressed by its first Secretary-General, the ICS should not be any more neutral on development problems than WHO's ICS on the drive to eradicate malaria (Weiss, 1986, pp. 88–89; see also Weiss, 1986, pp. 87, 96–97; Winslow, 1970, p. 215; Rasmusson, 1986, p. 110). There is no instrumentality involved in this, *eo ipso*. But the fact that the ICS dares not challenge the economic and trade policies of individual G77 countries, even though this could be argued to be useful from the viewpoint of common South (population) interests (Weiss, 1986; Ramsay, 1984) makes one wonder, if not the UNCTAD ICS is a good example of an instrumental relationship.[29]

If this is accepted, the UNCTAD ICS can also, however, illustrate a dilemma between the instrument role and that of mediation, as analysed by Weiss (1986, p. 90):

...the secretariat [ICS] has continuously vacillated between what are two incompatible roles. On the one hand, it has sought to be a 'prophet' for development thinking and issues, almost always taking the side of what might be described as the orthodoxy of Group of 77 thinking or at least not offending individual members of this group with proposals or ideas that went too far afield from their public stances. On the other, it has sought to be an active and non-partisan broker for negotiations attempting to stress realisable, not utopian, goals and having in mind the middle-ground for compromise required by developed countries.

Moreover, we do not exclude the possibility that an ICS can combine an instrument role in certain types of questions, with an autonomous role in other questions. The instrument role can also apply at the level of the individual civil servant, or as regards a certain office in an ICS (see Part II). The civil servant can be used by a certain IO member, typically the CS's country of origin, to promote its interests, generally or in certain specific issues.

The instrument role has been classified here as a political role; it should be obvious from the above, however, that it is not the ICS political values that it is believed to serve, but rather those of a particular IO member (- group).

The Substantial Roles

By 'substantial roles' are here understood the roles that are seen as means towards the IO/ICS substantial values. As already mentioned, however, these roles can also, if successfully carried out, be instrumental towards increased ICS prestige and hence the ICS political values (see Figure 2).

IO Identity supporter   The purpose of this role is to sustain the safeguarding of the IO values, through a PR effort for these values (that is, the IO's *raison d'être*) and for the IO in member-countries' populations.[30] If successful, this should deprive member governments of 'domestic arguments' for not being IO enthusiastic.

The identity role may be carried out by a particular 'information office' (or similar label), and typically also the Head of the ICS through his public announcements and visits to member countries (Rovine, 1970, p. 447; Jordan, 1979, p. 262). Also, as was mentioned initially, the very *existence* of an ICS, employed by and paid by the IO in question, serves to underpin the IO identity. In fact, it is the only permanent body that can provide such an underpinning to the IO's rather fragile identity. The EC Commission is probably the best example to mention here. Unlike the UN and NATO, who have 'only' identification actors in member countries, the EC has its own 'information agencies' physically located in member countries, in line with its more supranational character. This information activity has probably been most important, and controversial, in a country like Denmark, where membership *eo ipso* of the EC remained a political issue a long time after the Danish entrance in 1973.

The two closely related roles of conflict prevention and IO identity support both imply a certain penetration of the domestic political systems of IO member countries (in particular the former, see p. 15). This requires, almost as a necessary precondition, that these political systems are reasonably pluralistic. As expressed by Jönsson (1986, p. 44):

> The ability of an international organization... to reach into, and bring pressure to bear within, a given country depends on access to – and intelligence concerning – influential domestic groups; in other words, it implies a pluralist polity.

Cox (1973, p. 180) has also expressed views on this.

Initiator The role as initiator implies that the ICS proposes its own ideas to member-countries' representatives in the various IO committees. As stipulated here, we are not referring to proposals that are part of a mediation attempt (active mediation, see above), but proposals that are believed simply to further the substantial values of the IO. As with active mediation, this role requires a good deal of creativity, expertise, or authority on the part of the ICS. Generally speaking, the most typical initiators in IO committees are, of course, representatives of the most powerful member countries (Jordan, 1979, p. 257).

The best example of an ICS initiator is the EC Commission. According to the Treaty of Rome, the right to initiate EC action resides almost exclusively with the Commission, not with member countries.[31]

ICS initiation can also be found at more modest levels. Regarding the implementation process, it may amount to the prescription or suggestion of rules (guidelines) for the process that will, normally, be accepted by member countries. As to the preparation of meetings, we may find ICS initiation regarding agenda setting. The ICS agenda proposal will often be automatically accepted by member-countries' participants. To this could be added the identification and collection of 'relevant' information and background material for meetings, including the writing of reports and the invitation of special experts to the meetings (Eriksen, 1967, pp. 45–46, 53–57). In all these regards, the possession of the Chairman post in the relevant committee by the ICS will be a crucial advantage (as opposed to a rotation of this post among IO members). This pertains also, obviously, to the opportunities for suggesting specific proposals that were mentioned above.

What has been said here about initiation in the various phases of the process applies also to the closely related role of active mediation. For instance, a meeting agenda may come out as the result of an active mediation effort from the committee chairman, the ICS representative.

Operator/ controller/ observer As already mentioned, certain IOs have staff for implementing their decisions. As an example of such an *operative* role could be mentioned fieldwork in connection with the implementation of assistance projects in developing countries (for example, Bennett,1988, chapter II), or peace-keeping missions in areas of military conflict (for example, Bennett, 1988, chapter 7 or Skogmo, 1989).

If, in contrast, member countries themselves implement the common decisions, the ICS may function in the role as *controller*, that is, control that implementation is carried out in accordance with the aims, decisions and procedures of the IO. IAEA, for instance, controls that countries having signed the Non-Proliferation Treaty, and not already in the possession of nuclear weapons, do not use their peaceful nuclear technology for military purposes. This IAEA inspection is allowed in return for technical assistance programmes (Smith, 1987).

Evidently, control can be made with more or less rigour; there is no clear border line between control and what is merely *observation*, where the ICS simply registers the national implementation, without the willingness or ability to interfere, even if the implementation should be seen as unsatisfactory. This is the most widespread of the three implementation roles for ICSs (for example the UN impotence in relation to the follow-up of its many idealistic Assembly resolutions).

Expert/coordinator Certain international civil servants are employed by virtue of a particular expertise that is seen as crucial to the safeguarding of the IO substantial values. This expertise, be it in meteorology or medicine, can be relevant in any of the phases of decision-making, and it can be a precondition for certain of the roles stipulated above. Connected to the expert role will typically be advisory assistance to clients and member countries and independent design of directives, for example, for the implementation process.

A particular type of expertise is needed in coordination,[32] here referring to the avoidance of inconsistencies (standardization) or activity duplications (versus *political* coordination, that is, mediation, see above).

IO Representative vis-à-vis *non-members* An ICS may be allowed by its authority, the IO members, to represent the IO *vis-à-vis* non-members, in order to safeguard common interests. Normally, this will only happen in rather limited areas, or as regards already powerful ICSs. Typically, members will fear being lumped with (foreign policy) views that they do not share.

An example could be the EC Commission, carrying out trade and tariff negotiations with non-members, and conducting exploratory talks with states seeking associate status with the EC. Also, the Commission participates at such formal occasions as the receiving of ambassadors to the EC.

How Much Influence is Exerted?

As will be shown in Part III, an ICS can play different roles not only in various issue areas, but also within one and the same area.

By playing one or more roles, the ICS contributes to the modification of other actors' behaviour; in other words, it exerts influence, as this concept has been defined. How *much* influence can, evidently, only be assessed in very rough outline. *Ceteris paribus*, the more roles are played, the more influence is exerted, and as the roles have been stipulated, certain roles require more influence capability (exert more influence) than others. For instance, active mediation modifies the parties' positions more than does passive mediation, by definition. Among the bridge-building roles, the rank order seems to be the following: (1) conflict preventor, (2) active mediator, (3) passive mediator, and (4) communication facilitator. Among the implementation roles, the corresponding rank order is: (1) operator, (2) controller, and (3) observer. Among the substantial roles, the roles as initiator of proposals, operator and IO representative *vis-à-vis* non-members are those that require the most influence capability. The rank orders made here are those that can be made on the basis of definitions alone. More elaborate analyses of influence exerted can only be made in specific empirical cases, as we shall see in Part III.

The Environment Revisited: The Client/Authority Constellation and its Implications for the International Civil Service's Political Values

Having presented the ICS values, goals and roles, we shall now return to environmental relationships and their implications for the political values of the ICS.

Whereas the substantial values of the ICS were originally imposed by its authority (and hopefully internalized by the ICS), the political values will be mainly self-designed. This is so, in particular, as regards autonomy, that is, the ability to resist the influence of other actors, in this case the authority actors. Like any organization, autonomy is strived for by the ICS, but it is not likely to be enthusiastically or even voluntarily conceded by any authority worthy of its name. It is somewhat different with influence capability. As should appear from the feedback arrow in Figure 2 (p. 13), this capability can be used by the ICS to *exert* influence through the various roles. It can be used either to play the substantial or the political roles (or both), the latter being means towards a further increase in the ICS's own influence capability. Evidently, the authority (or most of it) prefers the former alternative: an ICS that seeks to promote the values that the IO was originally constructed to safeguard. A self-reinforcing sequence of feedback processes that gradually strengthens the ICS influence capability (and autonomy) is hardly in all authority actors' interest: they may feel that their own power and influence is infringed upon, in other words that they lose control. But they are seldom in a position to determine whether a given influence capability will be used by the ICS in a 'substantial' or a 'political' direction.

As an example of a self-reinforcing development could be mentioned the increased prestige and influence capability of the UN ICS in the wake of the UNEF success, contributing to the solution of the Suez crisis (see pp. 15–16). This led to further exertion of influence during for example the Congo crisis. This positive feedback development was brought to an effective halt by the Soviet Union, forcefully paralysing the UN ICS and particularly the Office of the Secretary-General, accusing its roles as initiator and active mediator for being played in a pro-Western way.[33] This reduced the influence capability of the UN ICS and hence both the substantial and political uses of it.

The question, how much autonomy and (self-reinforcing) influence capability that the ICS can manage to obtain, depends on several sets of factors.[34] One set has to do with the constellation of actors in its salient environment. In contrast to the other sets discussed this set is relevant both to a national and an international civil service. The catchphrase here, as it is for weak and dependent actors in general, is 'diversification of dependence'. The most unfavourable situation for the ICS is, of course, if there is no diversification at all: the authority is simultaneously a client, and the *only* client; hence, it stipulates the ICS's substantial values, provides the budget for their safeguarding, and as a client, it can closely supervise the quality of this safeguarding. Evidently, this constellation will leave little autonomy with the ICS (if any), and its influence capability will be used to promote substantial values, only. An example could be a secretariat performing service functions for the representatives of IO member countries only. The NATO IS is, to some extent, subject to this constellation, although, as we shall see in Part III, it tends to vary between issue areas of NATO activity (that is, between IS directorates).[35]

The constellation is more favourable if there are secondary clients, in particular if these are not in a position to complain to the IO authorities regarding poor service. This, of course, varies with their distance from government circles. Many UN specialized agencies, for instance, have clients that do not interact from a position of strength, being non-governmental recipients of aid. In such a constellation, more of the ICS influence capability can be used for its own political purposes, rather than 'wasted' in a substantial direction. The existence of identification actors, and absence of counter-groups and competitors will, of course, further improve the ICS position.

What really improves its position, though, is a diversification of budget sources. In other words, if not all of its budget originates from the authority, but some of it from clients or other sources, then a crucial diversification of dependence has been attained. This is the case, again, with many UN specialized agencies, which is one of the reasons why they have acquired such a relatively autonomous status, being insusceptible to coordination from above (McLaren, 1980b). One could also mention the EC's 'own incomes', being mainly a percentage of the basis of member-countries' value-added taxes, and customs duties on imports from third countries.[36]

To round off the subject of diversification (see, in general terms, Mintzberg, 1983, Part I and IV), there is reason to repeat the previous conclusion that IO harmony is beneficial to the ICS. In other words, unlike the other types of diversification mentioned here, diversification in the sense of disharmony between IO member countries (that is, the authority among itself), is *not* likely to be an advantage for the ICS – indeed, quite to the contrary.

The Need for Bridge-Building: Various Types of IO

I shall now argue that the need for bridge-building between IO member governments, that is, the need for the 'harmonizing' roles of conflict preventor, passive and active mediator, and communication facilitator, is likely to vary strongly between different types of IO. The following assumptions on the need for ICS bridge-building will be argued and explained below.

1. The less homogeneous the members of an IO in terms of ideology/type of society, the higher will be the degree of mutual conflict, and hence also the need for ICS bridge-building between them.
2. The higher the degree of pluralism in IO members' political systems, the more urgent will be the need for ICS bridge-building between IO members.
3. The more demanding the IO decision rules (for example, unanimity), the more urgent will be the need for ICS bridge-building between IO members.
4. The more implementation of IO decisions is left with members' civil services instead of its own ICS, and the less legal rights at the ICS's disposal, the more urgent will be the need for ICS bridge-building between IO members.

The four assumptions share the belief that expectations for a bridge-building effort will, at least to some extent, converge around the IO ICS. This, in turn, is based on the axiom that the ICS should be particularly qualified as a bridge-builder compared with other conceivable candidates such as nation states (for example, the IO members). Before we discuss each of the four assumptions, we should justify the axiom that they have in common.

First, the ICS has a selfish interest in IO harmony, as argued above. This should lead to higher energy and motivation than nation states would display in a bridge-building effort. The latter will hardly share the ICS's consistent interest in harmony; in a specific situation, some of them will be interested in harmony, whereas others will see certain substantial outcomes as the first priority – and vice versa in a subsequent situation.

Secondly, we should mention the role as IO identity supporter played by the ICS. This should give it a non-partisan image, so that its bridge-building will hardly be regarded as an attempt to win special advantages for itself (except for harmony *eo ipso*) – advantages that could later be turned against one of the contending parties.

Thirdly, the risk of dangerous linkages to other issue areas outside the fields of the IO is negligible – in contrast to the case of a national bridge-builder, simultaneously trying to safeguard a great many other interests. Fourthly, the ICS possesses a specialized expertise and information in the issue area(s) covered by the IO and should hence be assumed to be particularly constructive and imaginative in its bridge-building.

Finally, as already touched upon, and as expressed by Keohane and Nye (1974, p. 55):

> International secretariats staffed with knowledgeable individuals, even without traditional sources of power, have the opportunity to place themselves at the center of crucial communications networks, and thereby acquire influence as brokers, facilitators, and suggestors of new approaches.

Young (1967, pp. 113–114), in his somewhat more elaborate terminology than the one used here, agrees and adds some further arguments:

> ...the Secretary-General and the Secretariat may be better situated than most other potential third parties to play the role of intervener in terms of such factors as: 1) impartiality as between the principal parties; 2) salience [= prominence or uniqueness, *ibid.* pp. 83–84] in the eyes of the protagonists; 3) prestige and respect accorded to suggestions; 4) unity and ability to act coherently; 5) availability of diplomatic skill; and 6) the mobilization and coordination of actions.

This view, argued in some depth by Young, pertains to the UN ICS. However, the argument is so broad in its nature that it is hard to see why it should not be valid for ICSs in general.[37]

We shall now turn to the individual assumptions. The first one pertains to the *homogeneity* of member countries in its broadest sense, that is, in terms of ideology/type of society. The least homogeneous IOs are those with universal membership, that is, with members on both sides of the international bipolarity, and with both developing and industrialized countries as members. The underlying thought, then, is simply that heterogeneity entails a greater conflict potential than does homogeneity *ceteris paribus*. This is not only due to contrasting ideologies as such, but also to self-reinforcing suspicion *vis-à-vis* unknown and alien societies and cultures. The higher level of conflict will, in its turn, lead to a more urgent need for an ICS bridge-building effort, given the axiom outlined and explained above that an ICS is particularly well-suited to carry out the bridge-building roles.

The factor '*pluralism* in IO members political systems' comprises here two dimensions – both the number of countries with a pluralist system, and the degree of pluralism in these. The higher the degree of pluralism (dispersion of power), the more influence to clients, identification groups and, notably, counter-groups in the populations of IO members; this, in turn, causes the IO to be more vulnerable to popular trends in member countries with relevance for its field. One must always, for example, take the possibility into account that opposition parties, inspired by trends that run counter to the IO 'mainstream', form a cabinet after an election. This vulnerability cannot, of course, be reduced by the ICS, but it can pursue the kind of activities subsumed under 'conflict prevention' above. And as was noted on p. 20, these activities are in fact much easier to carry out in pluralist than in totalitarian societies. So taken together, pluralism is a double-edged sword from the viewpoint of the ICS: it creates an urgent need for conflict prevention, but this need is also made easier to fulfil.

A crucial parameter for any ICS is the kind of *decision-rules* followed by its IO (for example, Michelmann, 1978, pp. 13–14; Törnudd, 1982; or Lindell, 1987). The stricter the decision rules, the more vulnerable will the IO be *vis-à-vis* its members. The possibilities of neglecting existing conflicts/disagreements by deciding on the basis of simple voting majorities will be correspondingly reduced. Maximum vulnerability will be entailed by the principle of unanimity, where even the weakest member country can veto a decision proposal. The need for bridge-building will then be at a maximum: if only one member threatens to go its own way, bridge-building is needed between this member and the rest, if a decision is to be reached.[38] A double effect occurs if member countries are pluralistic and the IO decides on the basis of unanimity: the IO/ICS will then be hypersensitive to popular trends.

We have noted that the *implementation* of IO decision will often reside with members' bureaucracies, rather than with the ICS. Depending on the strength of the latter's controller role, members can omit the implementation of decisions not to their liking, implement them to a minor degree than they were intended by the IO, or in ways that distort their original intention (if any !) The implementation responsibility is, of course, an effective asset for members *vis-à-vis* the IO/ICS (Wallace, 1984, pp. 134, 140), in particular in the absence of any IO/ICS *legal powers* (and corresponding sanctions) to be used against non-complying members (which is, of course, the order of the day, except for the EC).[39] This means that the IO/ICS can hardly neglect a member's views; the member may only to a certain extent, or not at all, implement the decision (for example, Törnudd, 1982, pp. 172–173). To forestall this situation, bridge-building must also confer a certain minimum of acceptability to decisions for members that intend to vote against them.

The Environment, Values and Roles of the ICS 27

The Need for NATO International Civil Service Bridge-Building

We shall now evaluate the need for NATO ICS bridge-building, applying the general assumptions that were justified in the previous section.

First, the members of NATO are homogeneous, compared with other IOs – not least the universal ones, of course. Ideological homogeneity is almost taken for granted in NATO's Treaty (though not always a fact in the real world, see below). NATO *Facts and Figures* (1984, p. 264) state:

> They [the parties to this treaty] are determined to safeguard the freedom, common heritage and civilisation of their peoples, founded on the principles of democracy, individual liberty and the rule of law.

As to the intervening factor in the assumption, the degree of mutual conflict, NATO scores differently from what should be expected from homogeneity alone. Even though crisis rhetoric has been the order of the day since the establishment of NATO,[40] it can hardly be denied that a marked increase has occurred both in the frequency and intensity of conflicts/disagreements between member states in the course of the 1980s (for example, Sloan, 1986, chapter 6). The most salient conflict dimension has been the Atlantic one, that is, with the USA on the one side and most of the European allies on the other. In the wake of the 'New Cold War' between the Superpowers has followed Atlantic disagreements on questions such as the general relationship to the Soviet Union (continued strivings for *détente* ?), trade relations with the East (embargo ?), attitudes to arms control, and military burden sharing in the Alliance (the last, though, being a permanent subject for discussion). The fundamental reason for disagreement in these questions has been, like previously, divergent state interests, ultimately caused by different geographic locations in relation to the Soviet Union. In the 1980s, however, the European Allies have been more equal to the USA, economically and otherwise, than was the case during the first decades of the Alliance. Also a range of situation-specific factors have, undoubtedly, been of significance, both during the 'New Cold War' and during the subsequent *détente*. One can hardly argue that the number of challenges to harmony have waned with *détente*; consider, for instance, the disagreement on short-range nuclear missiles in 1989.[41] In addition to the conflict dimension described here, there are, of course, more specific ones, like the Greek/Turkish conflict that has existed for the whole lifetime of the Alliance, though with varying intensity.[42]

To sum up so far, we can observe that a significant need for bridge-building has existed among member states during the 1980s, though not for the heterogeneity reason mentioned in assumption (1) (see p. 24). This conclusion will be even more marked, when we consider the implications of the rest of the assumptions. As to assumption (2), we can say that NATO member countries, with the exception of Turkey, have been reasonably pluralistic during the

1980s, at least if seen in a global-comparative light. As to proposition (3), NATO's decision rules are the strictest that one can logically imagine: it is written in NATO's Treaty that decisions are made unanimously; that is, even the weakest member country has, formally, veto-power. And regarding proposition (4), the implementation of NATO decisions is to a very large extent left to member countries (see the further discussion in Part III). There are no NATO legal sanctions to be applied (for example, Taylor, 1978a). Such a crucial point as the content and size of defence budgets can only be recommended from NATO – they are decided upon and implemented nationally.

On the basis of this crude classification of NATO, the Alliance should actually reach a logical maximum as regards the need for bridge-building. It can be objected, of course, that the classification is of a formal nature. There exist measures in pluralist political systems to safeguard the 'broad consensus on national security policy' (or equivalent formulation), for example, a norm saying that matters of this type should be exempted from the turmoil of general party politics. Such a norm will, evidently, tend to reduce NATO vulnerability *vis-à-vis* unpredictable popular trends in member countries. Furthermore, it will have political costs, particularly for a weaker power to utilize the formal veto-power. The so-called 'footnotes' to NATO communiqués represent precisely a method for demonstrating a reserved attitude, without blocking a NATO decision (or statement).

To these objections can be replied, regarding the 'broad consensus', that this has actually cracked in a number of countries in the beginning of the 1980s (notably Denmark, Holland and Belgium – see Flynn, 1985; Ørvik, 1986). Some of NATO's issue areas have been strongly politicized in public opinions, in particular the nuclear field in the wake of the double-track decision of 1979. The peace movements (most of which qualify as 'counter-groups' in our terminology here) mobilized large segments of the populations up till about the middle of the 1980s, and they exerted a manifest influence in several countries on Social Democrat or Christian Democrat opposition parties.[43]

Regarding the question of footnotes, these are often regarded as negative events by NATO, due to their manifestation of a certain weakening of the Alliance 'solidarity' or 'unity', so carefully described in NATO communiqués. Bridge-building, for example, by the NATO ICS, can pre-empt or prevent footnotes.

Finally, from a *relative* point of view, that is, compared with other IOs, NATO must be characterized as hypersensitive *vis-à-vis* public opinions. It is hard to imagine an IO that could be classified more unambiguously in relation to our assumptions. NATO's need of bridge-building, hence, seems to be considerable.[44]

This need, evidently, poses an enormous challenge with the NATO ICS (or other conceivable bridge-builders like members themselves). It is not yet possible to establish expectations as to whether, to what extent, and how this challenge will be met by the ICS. This requires a knowledge, on the one hand, of the specific bridge-building needs in various issue areas and, on the other hand, of the ICS influence capability, in general and in the areas at stake. For instance, active mediation might well be needed in a given area, but capabilities only allow for the passive version of mediation.

Before we get to these area-specific analyses in Part III, however, we should focus on the general problem of self-control for the ICS. It will be argued, for example, that an insufficient degree of self-control is a threat to the ICS influence capability.

Notes – Introduction and Part I

1. As should appear, this is a minimalist definition. For an enumeration of 'characteristics' of an international organization, see Bennett (1988, pp. 2–3). See also, for example, McLaren (1980a, p. 1), or Rochester (1986, p. 778).
2. Throughout we consider organizations whose members are nation states (IGOs = International Governmental Organizations versus INGOs = International Non-Governmental Organizations). On INGOs in general, see for example Bennett (1988, chapter 16). On INGOs as crucial actors in the environment of IGOs and their civil servants, see p. 11 in this book.
3. The reasonings behind this stipulation are presented on p. 12.
4. To avoid sexism – 'he' or 'she' and so on – the international civil servant will be referred to as 'the CS' where appropriate.
5. The terms 'bureaucracy', 'administration', or 'secretariat' will, on a few occasions, be used instead of 'civil service' in this book.
6. 'Self-control' meaning the ICS's control over its own sub-units, both individual employees and offices (or whole departments, for that matter).
7. The closest parliamentary control with an ICS is that of the European Parliament with the EC Commission. However, it can in no way be compared with any national parliamentary control. See also Jacobson (1984, p. 129).

    The press is seldom interested in ICSs, although there have been a few 'scandals' in recent years that have found their way to the headlines (for example, concerning UNHCR in 1989). See further on p. 4.
8. The IGOs have been characterized as a kind of 'trade union of governments' (Galtung, 1986, pp. 2, 14), pertaining to the UN.
9. On the peculiarity question, in relation to a national service, see also Winslow (1970, p. 216), James (1971, p. 59), Bryde (1988) and Hilf (1988, pp. 213–214). McLaren (1980a, pp. 127–129), in one of the few systematic studies of the ICS, concludes that the differences between national and international civil services are more important than the similarities. See also Hansen (1975, p. 69):

    ...the comparisons that often are made, explicitly or implicitly, between national and international administrations, are more misleading than helpful. [Translated]

10. As expressed by Pitt and Weiss (1986, p. xi):

    while there is a growing literature on international problems and organisations, the perspective normally is on the politics or economics of issues and rarely on the dynamics of the people and structures charged with international co-operation.

30 The International Civil Service

Damsgaard (1983, p. 20) mentions that:

...international administration is underdeveloped (compared to the science of public national administration) as regards explicit theoretical foundations and conceptual models of analysis.

11. The authoritative journal *Public Administration Review* could provide another illustration: since 1970, when it published a special issue 'Towards an International Civil Service' (Mailick, 1970), it has contained three articles on the ICS: by Renninger (1977), Jordan (1981), and Reymond and Mailick (1986).
12. For a likely explanation for this, see p. 10 below. See also Jönsson (1986, p. 39).
13. Their source values vary a great deal (see the Appendix on Method, p. 133). Hoggart's memoirs (1978) from his time as an Assistant Secretary General in UNESCO should be emphasized here as an invaluable source to the internal life of an ICS. For a discussion of genres of ICS literature, see Gould and Kelman (1970).
14. See Pitt and Weiss (1986b, p. xi) or Ghebali (1986). Ramsay (1984, p. 394), himself an UNCTAD civil servant, concludes that:

Though established to help *poor countries*, UNCTAD has ended up by serving the interests of *rich people* [among them UNCTAD's own civil servants, according to the author]

15. The problems regarding secrecy, though, seem to be considerable also in an IO like the UN; see Pitt and Weiss (1986b, p. xii), or Pitt (1986, p. 25). See also the Appendix on Method (p. 133).
16. In this sense, Part III could be seen as a direct follow-up to the questions raised by James (1976). It should be mentioned, though, that James does not discuss ICSs as such, but IOs in broader terms. On IOs and ICSs as dependent and independent variables, respectively, see Cox (1973, pp. 156–157).
17. For Michelmann (1978, p. 47),

autonomy in the context of discussing a directorate general's performance means relative independence from council interference [that is, the member states] and a high degree of freedom to set norms with respect to its assigned policy area.

18. See also Dixon's (1981) classification of literature on the UN, being strongly biased in favour of stressing environmental explanatory factors (if considering the UN as an actor, in the first place).
19. Although it does not explain the scarcity of ICS studies. Michelmann's view is shared by Gordenker and Saunders (1978, p. 105), whose article is entirely dedicated to the question of the applicability of organization theory to the study of IOs and ICSs. It is concluded, for example, that:

International organisation can take on forms with which organisation theory has yet to come to grips, probably because of its emphasis on governments and business firms.

The forms referred to are, for instance, so-called 'para-organisations', that is, conglomerates of nationally stationed civil servants. McLaren (1980a, p. 127) states, similarly, that:

The obvious conclusion to this study is that the findings of public administration, concerning the secretariats of national governments, are not applicable to the secretariats of international organizations.

The views are argued by referring, for example, to the primacy of environmental explanatory factors.
20. There tends to be a certain overlapping between the categories at stake here: secondary clients will easily identify with the IO and its purposes (for example, agricultural organizations with the EC), and identification actors are also to a certain extent secondary clients, if their information activity is supported economically from the ICS (for example, the national 'Atlantic Associations' from NATO).
21. Only mention is made of the most crucial actors in the ICS environment. For more comprehensive lists of potentially relevant actors, see Jacobson (1984, pp. 99–100) or Harari and Bouza (1986, p. 50).
22. Though less self-control than a national civil service, as will be shown in Part II.
23. Michelmann's use of 'autonomy' (see Note 17) encompasses both influence capability and autonomy as here conceived. On these different conceptualizations, see Mouritzen (1988, p. 43, note 41).
24. One could, of course, think of counter-arguments to this whole reasoning on harmony. There are, for instance, the arguments in the 'tension between the strong, and the power of the weak' debate (Goldmann, 1979; Mouritzen, 1988, chapter 16; Mouritzen, 1990), the ICS being the weak (indeed the very weak!) and the IO member countries being the strong. Harmony seems both to favour and disfavour the weak, though in different respects: it strengthens autonomy, but it weakens influence capability. But this latter part of the argument does not hold water in the case of the 'very weak' (the ICS): it does not seem reasonable to assume that an ICS can actually play off the authority actors against each other, as a weak nation state may on occasions do with the stronger ones. And it does not seem that harmony will make the assets of the ICS superfluous – quite to the contrary.

One might also argue that the *need* for harmony is most urgent during disharmony and, hence, the need for a harmonizing effort from the ICS (see pp. 24–5). But the very need for an effort does not imply that the influence-capability to carry it out is available.
25. As to other typologies for the roles of ICSs or their clients, see Winslow (1970), Cox and Jacobson (1974, p. 12), or Michelmann (1978, p. 14). Rovine's (1970, pp. 440–463), typology of Secretary-General 'functions' is also relevant for the ICS as a whole; but it appears too heavily loaded with the abstract terminology of structural functionalism. None of the typologies mentioned here claim to be exhaustive.
26. The standard work on mediation and various intermediaries in international political crises is still Young (1967) I believe. As to mediation and related methods of peaceful settlement of disputes by IOs, see Bennett (1988, chapter 6, in particular pp. 101–103). Bennett does not distinguish between subtypes of mediation though.
27. As to passive and active mediation in a UN context, see Cox (1973, pp. 160, 176–179) (even though slightly different concepts are used). Haas (1964, p. 105) stipulates among his 'patterns of decision' two types that resemble our mediation categories here: 'deciding on the basis of the least common denominator of acceptability to the participants' (= passive mediation), and 'transforming the conflict by upgrading the participants' demands, that is discovering a higher level in which all parties are on agreement' (= active mediation). See also Gordenker and Saunders (1978, p. 91). Rovine (1970, p. 416) hints at the distinction, when saying that:

Neutrality has not always meant, however, a simple posture somewhere between the two antagonists. It is possible for a Secretary-General to remain neutral in a dispute by standing on Charter principles rather than between the narrowly defined political and military interests of the parties....

Strangely enough, he never conceptualizes the difference. The same goes for Cox and Jacobson (1974, p. 13).

28. A useful indicator of instrumentality could be that the ICS not only happens to serve the interests of one particular member (-group), but also manifestly counteracts the official IO purposes that it should work for. This is not so by definition though.
29. The instrumentalist philosophy has been expressed by W. Michael Blumenthal (1988, p. 529), as cited from Väyrynen (1989), pertaining to the US and post-war economic ICS/IOs:

    We created new international institutions, and by and large, they did what they should.

    Probably, though, the paintbrush is somewhat broader here than it actually should be.
30. As to the internal functions of these values (that is, within the ICS), see pp. 50–1.
31. Of course, other actors may induce the Commission to act, although such inducement remains in the realm of persuasion (Michelmann, 1978, p. 13). The World Bank should also be emphasized for its initiating role, compared with other ICSs (Crane and Finkle, 1981; Ascher, 1983, p. 436).
32. On coordination conceived as rationalization (= the process of attempting to remove duplication of activities between or among units), standardization, and priorization, see McLaren (1980b).
33. The Secretary General forcefully defended his Office and the very concept of an ICS in a famous lecture in 1961 (Hammarskjöld, 1971).
34. We shall remember that ICSs have been stipulated as coherent and stable organizations in their own right, thereby singling them out from mere aggregates of nationally stationed civil servants (for example, 'para-organizations'). But for the ICS category, we do not distinguish dichotomously between those that are 'bureaux', and those that are not (Downs, 1967, pp. 24–31). As should appear, we merely operate with *degrees* of autonomy and influence capability. As to the reasons for this, see Note 35.
35. Still, in Downs' conceptualization, the NATO IS would qualify as a bureau: (1) it is large, (2) its employees are full-time workers who depend upon their employment in the organization for most of their income, (3) hiring and promotion of personnel is, to a certain minimum extent, based on merit (as opposed to religion, race, etc.) and (4) its output is not directly or indirectly evaluated in any markets external to the organization. However, we can hardly expect typical bureau behaviour from the NATO IS. One of the reasons for this is precisely its somewhat unfavourable client/authority constellation described in the text. Serving the authority directly may have the same anti-bureau effects as the market is believed to have in Downs' conception (the money flows from the primary client/customer) (see Mintzberg, 1983, chapter 18 or Larsen, 1986, p. 26). Hence, we shall avoid a sharp distinction between bureaux and non-bureaux in this book.
36. In fact, already the ECSC was allowed its own finance in the 1950s from a tax directly levied on the coal and steel industries of member countries (Taylor, 1978b, p. 220).
37. Young, though, does not include the ICSs of regional IOs in this argument (*ibid.* pp. 105–108).
38. It is a commonly held view in the literature on IOs and small states that (Jacobson, 1984, p. 126):

    …the formal voting procedures of international governmental organizations give small, weak and poor states resources that they would not otherwise have

    Galtung (1986, pp. 3–4) describes the IOs as 'social democratic' in this respect, that is, redistributive in favour of the weak *ceteris paribus*.
39. See further on p. 75.
40. See for example some of the contributions to Myers (1980).
41. Hence, rather than the level of tension between the Superpowers, it seems that the occurrence of turbulent events is a crucial factor for NATO harmony. And such can occur as well during high tension (for example, the introduction of Martial Law in Poland 1981),

42. as during *détente* (for example, the political transformations in Eastern Europe 1989–1990).
42. Not to mention the specific problems connected to French membership of the Alliance since about 1960. These problems, however, have only played a modest role during the 1980s.
43. And possibly also a latent influence on parties in government. As regards the United States, the threat to NATO cohesion has come from rather amorphous, isolationist trends in public opinion, trends that are in no way novel. But they have never been allowed to play a manifest role in Washington.
44. But it is not an official purpose of NATO to solve member conflicts (cf. the Treaty), in contrast to a collective security arrangement like OAS (see Vandevanter, 1970, p. 97). Means to solve member conflicts are mentioned, though, in the 'Report of the Committee of Three...' from 1956 (that happened to be published during the Suez Crisis, implying the most serious NATO disharmony since the establishment of the Alliance).

Part II How International is the International Civil Service ?

> It is not so much that the political pressure is intense but that our resistance is so low (interview statement by a UN personnel officer (Weiss (1982), p. 301).

The Problem of Internationalism for the International Civil Service: The Nature of the Problem

It was argued in the Introduction that among a range of peculiarities of the international civil service (ICS) *vis-à-vis* a national service, the most essential one was probably the extent of the problem of self-control for the ICS (that is, its problem of internationalism). Therefore, we shall dedicate the whole of Part II to this problem, its causes and implications, and what may be done about it, if one wishes.

Self-control, that is, controlling sub-units' behaviour, is likely to be a problem for all large, allegedly hierarchical organizations. Moreover, as expressed by Downs (1967, p. 262; see also chapter XII):

> The greater the effort made by a sovereign or top-level official to control the behavior of subordinate officials, the greater the efforts made by those subordinates to evade or counteract such control.[1]

In addition to this general tendency, however, the problem of self-control is reinforced for the ICS, because its salient environment consists of the world's, by far, most powerful actors, that is, nation states. They are its authority actors, as described in Part I. The international civil servants are recruited from them, typically from their civil services. Member governments of the IO wish, as part of their general striving for prestige and reputation, to fill as many posts as possible in the ICS with their nationals. Also, though to varying degrees, they wish to control or influence them subsequently. This is facilitated by the fact that member governments have delegations of their civil servants attached to the major IO Headquarters (see further discussion on p. 52). The means of influence range from 'instructions' proper, to subtler means, based on anticipated reaction (that is, the civil servants anticipating what their country 'probably' wants) or identification (that is, civil servants identifying themself with their country or its policies).

The counterweight to government influence, in one or the other form, for individual civil servants, is the fact that they are employed by, and paid by, the ICS/IO. The oath that is included in the UN Staff Regulations, and copied by many IOs, that is relevant in present context, is as follows (cited from Damsgaard, 1983, p. 206):

> I solemnly swear (undertake, affirm, promise) to exercise in all loyalty, discretion and conscience the functions entrusted to me as an international civil servant of the United Nations, to discharge these functions and regulate my conduct with the interests of the United Nations only in view, and not to seek or accept instructions in regard to the performance of my duties from any Government or other authority external to the Organization.

What is at stake here is the very concept of an impartial ICS, serving the IO member countries in an independent way. The ideal of such a service has existed since the establishment of the League of Nations and its Secretariat after World War I (Dublin, 1983). It should be mentioned here that this ideal has not always been respected by all members of the League/UN, not even rhetorically: this goes for Italy and Germany in the inter-war years, and the Eastern Bloc after World War II, that is, the countries with the most emphasis on centralized control in their own societies and hence, also with 'their' international civil servants.[2] Other member-countries have paid lip-service to the ideal, but have not respected it in actual fact (for example, the United States).[3] It is generally accepted in the literature on ICSs that the ideal is regularly infringed upon, more by some governments, though, than by others (James, 1971, p. 67; Reymond and Mailick, 1986, p. 138). Hoggart (1978), a former ASG in the UNESCO ICS, notes in his memoirs:

> ...relationships between the Secretariat [ICS] and the bulk of Permanent Delegates are not happy: there are too many attempts to lean heavily from one side and too much nervous readiness to yield on the other [p. 73]

> In short, and more brutally, they expect loyalty and leaks. The pressures on some Secretariat members can be so constant that they cease to feel like pressures and become an accepted aspect of the job. Many secretariat members are simply

required, by their Delegations, always to have in mind the interests of their countries, to tell all and to act in the way they are told...[p. 115]

It should, of course, be remembered that the overwhelming majority of the ICS activities, being of a routine character, do not raise problems. But there is consensus among authors on ICSs that when dealing with important issues, the extent of the problem of self-control is peculiar to the ICS, compared with a national service (Reymond and Mailick, 1986, p. 137):

> It [the independence of the service, with its cognate requirement of primary loyalty to the organization] is correctly seen as the cornerstone of the nature of the service. It raises recurrent controversies on the question whether international civil servants are actually guided by the principles and policies of the organization they serve or by those of their home countries.

What may be subject of disagreement is rather the *implication* of this peculiarity. In other words: is it actually a *problem* for the ICS/IO, and for international cooperation in broader terms? This will now be discussed.

Is it a Crucial Problem?

It is my view that ICSs, IOs and international cooperation in the relevant field would function better if ICSs' self-control (internationalism) were improved. The argument runs as follows: the more influence that countries exert over their nationals in an ICS, the more it will get the character of a multi-national conglomerate rather than an international institution with its own interests and actor properties and influence. The ICS's internal life will be dominated by (national) conflicts of interest and ensuing mutual suspicion and control. Young (1970, p. 228) argues that national influence and pressure

> ...may still further indirectly undermine it [the ICS integrity] by opening him [the Secretary General] or the Staff to the suspicion of being subject to pressure even when they are not. It further has a cumulative effect, namely that other governments may through the force of imitation or deliberately as a counter-measure act in a similar way, thus completely undermining the confidence in the international civil service.

In other words: the problem of internationalism is self-reinforcing.[4]

The proposals that the ICS will be able to make in committees, as part of member-country mediation or in attempts to play other roles, will be an expression of a lowest (national) common denominator. This follows from the mutual watchfulness, or even suspicion. In other words, the ICS will not be able to propose new bold ideas (as a 'think tank'), or new ideas in the first place. They will probably be 'vetoed', in pseudo-impartial terms, of course, but in actual fact due to national influence. Or they may not even be put on paper or articulated, in the anticipation that it is no use anyway. The 'fights' that should theoretically take place between the proper national representatives in the various IO committees, have already been fought (or suppressed) in advance, within the walls of the ICS. The ICS will almost get the characteristics of a committee, as described by Vandevanter (1970, p. 112):

> Whereas committees... can argue over and make modifications to a plan drawn up elsewhere, they are generally unable to provide the homogeneity in outlook that is necessary to *draft* plans for dealing with complex problems.

The ICS, hence, will not be creative. The cautious suggestions that the ICS might still be able to come up with, will be met with suspicion by governments, or at least some of them. May the ICS be running the errand of one particular member country? Is the particular office of the ICS known to be an instrument of certain interests? The ground will be fertile for paranoia, and the 'safest' member attitude will be seen as a reserved attitude to the (cautious) ICS proposals.

Taken together, we can say that a high degree of national influence on the ICS employees, that is, a low degree of ICS self-control, will reduce the ICS creativity and its ability to exert influence on member governments. Hence, the ICS will be inhibited from playing the most ambitious, influential roles such as conflict prevention, active mediation and initiator. To express it inversely, improved self-control for the ICS entails improved influence capability (proposition 1 in Figure 3.)[5]

Even if ICS creativity and influence do not constitute the only keys to fruitful international cooperation,[6] the lack of ICS self-control, according to this reasoning, constitutes a genuine problem to international cooperation. So if one, from a normative point of view, wishes to strengthen international cooperation, then one should, for example, seek to strengthen ICSs' self-control.

Could and Should Something be Done About the Problem?

In Figure 3, a range of propositions on the causes and implications of ICS self-control (internationalism) have been illustrated. They lay the ground for a prescriptive orientation; by manipulating the assumed causal factors in a certain direction, one can reduce, and theoretically eliminate, the problem of ICS self-control, if one so wishes. What this direction amounts to will be discussed and analysed below.

There is a second set of causal factors also, pertaining to those in a position to manipulate the causal factors above, that is, IO member governments. We shall return, briefly, to this set later (pp. 60–1).

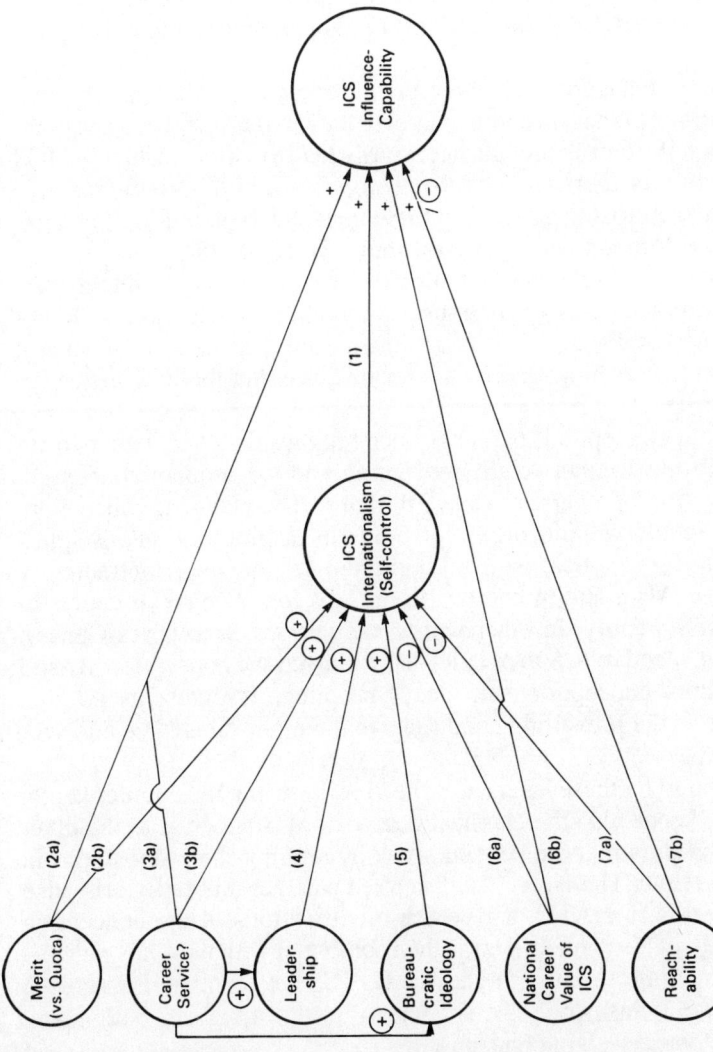

Figure 3 A model of factors determining ICS internationalism (self-control) and the implications of these for ICS influence capability

The figure is based on the counterweight conception of ICSs described in the text. The arrows indicate assumed causal relationships (of a positive (+) or a negative (−) nature)

The propositions in Figure 3 are not all undisputed. Together, they constitute what we here label the '*counterweight conception*' of ICS self-control. It amounts to a clarification and minor modification of the so-called '*classical*' *conception* of the ICS, adhered to, mainly, by practitioners (for example, Secretary-Generals in their memoirs) and certain academic writers.[7] The essence of the conception is that IOs, in order to be influential and sustain international cooperation, should establish a certain (modest) counterweight to governments' pressures, by virtue of strengthened institutions. Their civil servants should be employed by the Head of the IO on the basis of merit (primarily). The ICS should be a career service and its structure formally hierarchical, just like a national administration. These characteristics and some further ones, should protect the international civil servants from national encirclement and pressure.

As we shall see later, there are both practitioners and scholars who will dispute proposition (1) that was argued above: they will argue that a strengthening of the ICS self-control does not necessarily lead to a more influential ICS – quite to the contrary (here labelled the '*resignists*'). The IO/ICS must live with, and resign itself to, the national encirclement and exploit the advantages that it can also be argued to entail (for example, Simai, 1978).

A third school of thought, here labelled the '*utopians*', argue that even if governments' embracements and pressures should be avoided, this should not happen by strengthening the ICS as an institution. The means for such a strengthening have harmful side-effects, for instance that the ICS stiffens in bureaucratic inertia.

Among the four conceptions that have been roughly sketched here, two are ideal types: both the counterweight conception and the utopian conception imply the cultivation of a certain way of thinking. The classical conception, from where the counterweight conception draws its inspiration, is not an ideal type, as it argues for practical/political compromises between contradictory ways of thinking. Also, and in contrast to the two former ones, it claims to represent empirical reality; in other words, the various Secretaries-General argue that their respective ICS in practice has followed the conception, by and large.[8] The resignist conception is no ideal type, either: it represents, *eo ipso*, an acquiescence in the prevailing conditions that nation states have allowed, that is, status quo.

As already hinted by these labels, it is the view here that the counterweight conception (and hence also the classical conception) is superior to the other ones. This can be shown at the general level, by arguing the propositions in Figure 3, one at a time. Then it will be discussed whether this superiority also applies with regards to NATO, and which modifications of the conception might be required in this context. This is then compared with what has *actually* been done, if anything, to improve the NATO ICS self-control. Finally, we consider if governments would be willing to accept a reform built upon, essentially, the counterweight conception.

The Relevant Propositions

The Principle of Merit versus Quota

A principle that is stressed in the classical conception of the ICS is the principle of merit in the recruitment (and promotion) of personnel. This means simply that one employs the best qualified candidate to a given position, regardless of attributes in other respects. One must not take into consideration any forms of quotas, be they based on nationality or other criteria (sex, age, and so on)

Proposition (2b) in Figure 3 shall now be argued, that is, that the principle of merit improves the ICS's self-control or, inversely, that national quotas increase international civil servants' dependency homewards. Firstly, national quotas, in the form of 'desirable ranges' of employees for each country, be they openly admitted or not, are symbolically unfortunate, because they express a representational way of thinking. Individual civil servants contribute to the filling of their own country's quota. The symbolic implications of this may lead to further national encirclement. This could happen, for instance, if nation states gained a prescriptive right to certain positions that, consequently, would be inherited between fellow countrymen (criticized by de Cuellar, 1988, p. 94). It would be even worse, of course, if they gained the right to the domination of a certain office in the ICS.

A closely related risk would be if governments gained influence on the appointments of the people within its quota. If a government has got a too modest quota (which they almost all seem inclined to feel), then there is all reason to try to compensate for this by filling it up with 'reliable' people. The risk is, in other words, that the employees will be in a more or less amorphous debt of gratitude homewards. Their dependency in this direction will be correspondingly higher. As argued by Reymond and Mailick (1986, p. 139):

> Giving priority to nationality over competence inevitably exalts the role of governments in the recruitment process. It is an open secret that, for a number of nationalities, the door to UN service is not through the normal recruitment programs but through the permanent mission of one's country. Though its purpose is different, the UN nationality distribution scheme thus leads to a growing control by governments of a staffing process that, according to the Charter, is the exclusive province of the executive head; this gives governments excessive power over the initial and subsequent administrative fate of their nationals in the secretariat.

Or as expressed by Modelski (1970, p. 211), pertaining to the recruitment policy of SEATO, based entirely on national selection:

> ...the current policy leaves too much of the recruitment in the hands of those who are not responsible for the work and maximizes opportunities for political and private pressures.

So much can be said in support of proposition (2b). As with proposition (1), a crucial argument is that of a self-reinforcing mutual suspicion between governments: it is important not to be worse off than the others, who have probably found 'reliable' people to fill their quotas.[9]

If we trust proposition (1), we have now made it probable that national quotas decrease the influence capability of the ICS. There is also, however, a proposition (2a, see Figure 3) pointing to a *direct* relation between the two factors. The reasoning is simple: the principle of merit will entail that the ICS will come to consist of the most competent civil servants. Or negatively stated, it avoids the 'deadwood' (as jargon mercilessly calls them) that is often said to be a consequence of national quotas: several countries will not be able to fill up their quotas with reasonably competent people (James, 1971, p. 66; Wells, 1986, pp. 150–151); other countries have competent candidates, but will use the ICS as a kind of 'dumping ground' (again the jargon) for people, who are 'difficult' (for example, political opponents) or with questionable competence (James, 1971, p. 62). As argued by Hoggart (1978, pp. 47–48; see also p. 116), pertaining to UNESCO:

> ...the case against geographical spread as it is at present practised is weighty. Some nations employ their staffing range as a useful form of patronage, or a convenient refuge for the otherwise unplaceable. It is harder for the Director General to resist the claims being made for the Minister's cousin, whom he knows to be lazy and corrupt, if the Minister's country is underrepresented.... Such elaborate formalities in making appointments through a series of complex maneuvers not mainly connected with the needs of a particular job are probably common to the internal procedures of more States than not; so this is the way they will act, whatever an IO's Regulations may say... .

If less competent people have been recruited for quota reasons, perhaps even selected by a certain government, they are also difficult or impossible to get rid of for the ICS; the countries they 'represent' will feel that their prestige has been hurt. The only way out will typically be, as expressed by Cox (1973, p. 167), to

> ...maneuver them out of the executive circuit of communication within the bureaucracy.

but even this can cause resistance from the government in question.

To this could be added that quotas in connection with promotions may demoralize the civil servants who feel passed over due to their nationality, in favour of a demonstrably less qualified candidate (Michelmann, 1978, p. 28). Taken together, an ICS with less qualified and demoralized civil servants, even though only a minority, will not be able to function creatively, or to further proposals that can win adherence by member countries.[10] If the ICS's general reputation among governments has been damaged, it will be difficult to exert very much influence on them.

As a further argument, any forms of quotas will increase the rigidity of the ICS. It will lead to endless discussions on which quota criterion is most 'fair'.[11] At each appointment or promotion, an arithmetic equation will have to be solved, an equation that can even be solved by different formulae. Another type of rigidity is entailed, if certain offices are regarded as the 'sphere of interest' of a certain country or bloc. They will then be very difficult to abolish, even if the ICS should so wish (Meltzer, 1978, p. 1015, cited from Damsgaard, 1983, p. 84):

> ...reorganization efforts are more likely to lead to parallel or circumventing structures rather than dismantling existing bodies.

The result is the accumulation of redundant structures in the ICS.

The types of rigidity mentioned here will, of course, weaken the ICS creativity and, hence, influence capability. As increased rigidity follows from the national quotas, our belief in proposition (2b) must be strengthened: that national quotas decrease the ICS influence capability.

NATO: Merit versus quota[12] As with the EC and UN ICSs, the principle of merit is only applied within narrow limits in the NATO IS. That each member country has a highly unofficial quota of employees (a 'desirable range') entails that it is seldom possible to hire the best qualified candidate. NATO's first Secretary-General formulated the problem in the following way (cited from Jordan, 1967, pp. 145–146):

> It is perhaps not sufficiently realized that the NATO International Staff suffers from certain inherent handicaps... it is obviously desirable that all member countries should be proportionately represented on the Staff. Consequently there can be no question of international competitive bidding for appointments. These have to be allotted not to the best man available in the Alliance, irrespective of nationality, but to the man selected by the government of the particular country which, in the interest of proportionate representation, is asked to fill the appointment in question.

This is an example of the mechanism previously indicated that a quota arrangement leads to national appointments. However, things have changed since then, by virtue of Lord Ismay's own efforts, among other things (Jordan, 1967, pp. 145–151). The system was changed so that *several* delegations were asked (selected after the quota system) to present candidates, and so that the selection among these should be made by NATO on the basis of merit.

This seems, by and large, to be the way the system functions today (i 1, i 2, i 3, i 7) (i = interview). Lord Carrington (1988, p. 381) describes the system in his memoirs:

> An important post on the International Staff may become vacant. It demands to be filled by a candidate of quality. It also demands to be filled by a candidate who is

not from countries A and B, who filled the last four such posts – and who now present by far the best qualified two candidates. NATO staffing as well as NATO policy can absorb a good deal of time, and on every occasion when such a job is on offer each NATO Ambassador visits the Secretary-General to explain that his country is underrepresented on the International Staff, and that he has the pleasure of now proposing an outstanding, no doubt the only outstanding, name.

In other words, within the narrow limits set by the quota system, merit is allowed a certain role. It should be added that the quota system is applied not only on the NATO IS as a whole, but also all the way down to the level of sections (i 12, i 18). In a section with eight employees, there exists an 'invisible upper limit' (i 18) of two or three employees of the same nationality. The example is from such a technical and, hence, merit-needing field as infrastructure, where it should *a priori* be expected that one would be more large with dispensations from quotas than elsewhere.

The weight that is ascribed to the filling of vacancies on the part of delegations can be deduced from the fact that more than one Secretary-General has described appointments as the most difficult of his tasks whatsoever (i 12), even though we are only talking about fixed-term appointments. Even Royal Heads have been mobilized by states at such appointments (i 4). We shall return to the possible *reasons* for this strong engagement on the part of delegations and governments.

The Existence of a Career Service

The classical conception insists that the ICS must be a career service (for example, Hammarskjöld, 1971, pp. 261–262). This implies, for the civil servants, the possibility of a life-long service (as opposed to fixed-term contracts), and also the opportunity of advancing vertically through the system to the highest posts. In this connection should also be mentioned other benefits like a reasonable job security, a salary that is competitive with the highest national civil servants' salaries, and a pension system.

Proposition (3b) says that the more an ICS resembles a career service (a question of degree), the better will be its self-control. In other words: the less will be individual civil servants' dependency homewards. The argument, being based on our previous assumptions of a general nature (p. 12), is also founded on Downs' proposition (1967, p. 262; also chapter XVII), saying that

> All officials exhibit relatively strong loyalty to the organization controlling their job security and promotion [providing a career service].

The positive sanctions inherent in a career service will improve civil servant loyalty, and function as a counterweight to the advantages that will always be implied by service in one's own country.[13] The anxious glances homewards for a future position in the national bureaucracy that are a consequence of a fixed-term contract will be unnecessary (Mathur, 1986, pp. 175–176; see also, in general, James, 1971, p. 70; Reymond and Mailick, 1986, p. 138).

Even though an ICS, in principle, has a career service as described here, one cannot be sure that it functions as such in practice. It may be as in the UN, where top post vacancies are almost always filled from outside, so that very few of the ICS's own people see a chance of reaching the top.[14] This makes it reasonable to regard the question of career service as one of degree. As implied by Downs, the more vertical mobility in an ICS, the more identification with it and hence resistance to outside pressure.

Proposition (3a) also assumes a *direct* link from the question of career service to the ICS influence capability (see Figure 3). A high vertical mobility makes it possible to recruit and retain the best civil servants and this entails, as we have seen, a more influential ICS. Another beneficial consequence flowing from a career service is continuity (for example, Bennett, 1988, p. 391). In contrast to a system of fixed-term contracts, the ICS gets a 'memory' for a longer time-span. It is to be avoided that civil servants, having learned the routines of the job and established the necessary contacts, and so on, will after about one year of service jump to other employment in order not to find themselves unemployed at the expiration of their fixed-term. A CS's successor will then have to start from scratch in learning the working routines (if there is somebody to teach the CS). It must be assumed that the gain in continuity flowing from a career service implies an obvious gain in effectivity in daily work, and consequently it also contributes to ICS influence capability.

The career service has further beneficial effects for the ICS, through some of the factors that we shall deal with below.

NATO: Career service? NATO's IS does not, unlike the EC Commission, constitute a career service. The IS has a mixture of individual contracts and a system of secondments, implying that the civil servants are temporarily on leave from their home service. The typical duration of an appointment is three to five years, although it tends to vary a great deal. Promotions are infrequent, and then typically within rather technical fields (i 1, i 12), where it may be possible to attain a life-long career. This is, however, the exception. NATO has, obviously, a 'policy of big turnover' (i 7).

For the seconded civil servants, it is easy to imagine a potential conflict of loyalty between NATO and the government that the employee is expecting to return to. As expressed by one Director (i 7):

...my superior's assessment of me is relatively unimportant. To me, the important thing is, what [my capital] thinks about me...

The filling of top-post vacancies from outside does, on occasion, cause demoralization in the Staff (Jordan, 1967, p. 151). To this could be added that in periods where the IS salaries have not been able to follow the highest national civil servant salaries, the level of qualifications for the seconded civil servants has been lowered, not surprisingly. In the judgement of Jordan (1967, pp. 124–125), such a development has also been a source of demoralization among those already employed.

We shall return to the implications of this lack of career service in connection with the discussion of reform proposals for the NATO IS.

The National Career Value of an ICS employment

The national career value of an ICS employment[15] is crucial, as a large part of international civil servants are recruited from, and return to, national bureaucracies. The higher the value, the more competent people will be recruited and the more they will be motivated to do their very best in general terms, and to be 'loyal' to their home country (or in any case not disfavour it in any matter). With low national career value, it is less likely that anyone at home will bother about their work, neither in general terms, nor in national terms.

Seen from the viewpoint of the ICS, the risk of encirclement of its employees is lowest in the latter case. But, on the other hand, the ICS does not get as competent people as in the former case. Or to put it inversely: high national career value of the service creates a risk of low ICS self-control (proposition 6a in Figure 3); on the other hand, the ICS gets competent people and will, hence, be more effective and influential than with low national career value (proposition 6b).

It should be added here that the national career value tends to vary between member governments of an IO, and also between bureaucracies within one government.

The National Career Value of a NATO IS employment

In the Danish Foreign Ministry, the career value of a NATO IS employment is low, or perhaps even negative. This is expressed in all interviews with a clarity and distinctness that is rather unusual for civil servants (i 1, i 2, i 3, i 5, i 8).[16] The NATO employment can be a

- '...solution for a civil servant, who has got stuck in the national service' (i 1);
- 'it can be by way of consolation, but not a good consolation' (i 5);
- 'a corresponding number of years will be wasted in a national career' (i 3);
- 'if you are gone for 3 or 4 years, you will be forgotten' (i 5).

A priori and naively, one should believe that some years of NATO service and the ensuing experience with multinational diplomacy, even close to national high politics, would be of obvious national career value. Which are the reasons, then, for the low reputation described above? One of them is inherent in the staffing policy of 'generalism', according to which all civil servants shall cover the whole diplomatic field, in principle; there are not seen to be resources for specialization in particular issue areas or regions (in case security policy). So the former NATO civil servant risks being transferred to matters on South East Asia, instead of using the experience in the Foreign Ministry 'NATO Office'.[17] This may be the CS's own wish, though; in view of the prevailing staff policy, the CS may consider it necessary for career purposes to avoid a too narrow 'security' image, and therefore try to broaden it as in the example that was mentioned (i 43).

This in itself, however, can hardly be a full explanation. A period in the NATO IS could be regarded on a par with an ordinary embassy stationing and hence, *ceteris paribus*, entail good career value. Here, however, the principle of 'out of sight, out of mind' comes into the picture; this expression was actually used spontaneously by three interview persons (i 1, i 8, i 43). In other words: one risks being forgotten, and the relevant Heads' awareness of one's capabilities becomes foggy or disappears (in contrast to the NATO *delegations* that are in daily and intense contacts with their respective capitals). To this comes, then, the vicious circle: the lack of promotion incentives and the relatively low reputation entails that it is seldom the most qualified people that seek an IS appointment or, for that matter, other ICS appointments. Consequently, their general reputation is further reduced.[18]

The question is, can this Danish Foreign Ministry experience be generalized? Firstly, it does not apply uniformly to *all* types of IS positions (a position close to the Secretary-General seems to imply a good national career value, for example). Secondly, other Ministries have a more positive attitude than the Foreign Ministry to ICS appointments. Thirdly, transcending the Danish context, the perspective cannot be generalized to all Alliance countries; most important, it does not apply for a major Alliance country like the United States, permitting its Foreign Service people an extensive degree of specialization. A secondment to the NATO IS can be highly meriting for a Foreign Service career,

- '...provided that one does not stay too long' (i 14).
- 'They [the Foreign Service] send good people, and good people get good experience' (i 14).

However, it is the US, and not Denmark, that is the exception to the rule.[19] Generally speaking for the Alliance, the NATO IS employment has a rather low national career value, due among other things to the lack of specialization generally allowed in the Foreign Ministries. To illustrate the generality of our observations, in time and space, the memoirs can be cited of Dirk Stikker, NATO Secretary-General (1960–1964) and previously Dutch Foreign Minister (Stikker, 1966, p. 338):

My only complaint would be that some foreign offices tend still to think in terms of purely national administration. The result is that in some of the diplomatic services of the Alliance lengthy assignments to the Secretariat, that is, to the Alliance as such, as distinct from service to purely national aspirations, can tend to slow a man's progress in his career. This is not only unfair, it is shortsighted. The needs in the future for men and women who can work loyally and effectively in cooperative international ventures will be greater, not less.

Leadership

One of the main requirements in the classical conception of the ICS is that the formal structure of the ICS should be hierarchical, that is, that the individual civil servant refers to his immediate superior all the way up to the ICS leadership, just like the formal structure in a traditional national administration. This hierarchical structure should then lead to a reasonably hierarchical functioning, meaning that the ICS in practice approaches this idea – in other words, that leaders actually have a grip on what the ICS is doing. In this conception is included the view that the very top leadership should be of a unitary rather than collegiate type. This means, in practice, that the ICS should be headed by *one* international civil servant (a 'Secretary-General' or equivalent label) instead of several, more or less 'representing' countries or blocs within the IO (for example, like the EC College of Commissioners).

We need not address here the general discussion on the feasibility of effective hierarchical functioning (see Note 1). It should be possible to assert that leadership from above may, *ceteris paribus*, provide a certain bulwark for the ICS against external pressure. If there are no instructions from above, it should be easier to fall prey to external 'instructions'. Also, 'pep-talks' once in a while from the leadership, stressing the integrity of the ICS and the Staff Regulation prohibiting external instructions, might have some bulwark effect.

It also seems reasonable to assume, in line with the classics, that a unitary leadership can provide more explicit guidance than a collegiate one, where the lowest common denominator between the leadership constituents may prove to be a rather amorphous steering device. Moreover, if the leadership itself is regarded from a representational point of view (even though formally a unit), then its warnings against national encirclement will sound hollow and not very credible. The reasonings in the present section can be subsumed under proposition (4) in Figure 3, saying that leadership, and notably a unitary type of leadership, will contribute to increased ICS self-control, *ceteris paribus*.

We should also add the relationship between the question of career service and the effect of leadership. As already implied, one reason why leadership does not function may be the lack of a career service, giving the ICS few positive sanctions to offer its civil servants, who instead may be influenced by their home bureaucracies.

NATO: Leadership The NATO IS has a unitary type of leadership, a Secretary-General. Also, the IS has, formally speaking, a hierarchical structure. How much bulwark these two attributes can provide against external pressure is, however, dubious. Interviews seem to indicate that the actual functioning of the IS is not particularly hierarchical, and in any case varies much between Divisions. We shall distinguish between the leadership's *possibilities* and *willingness* to lead the Staff, and the *necessity* of such *leadership*.

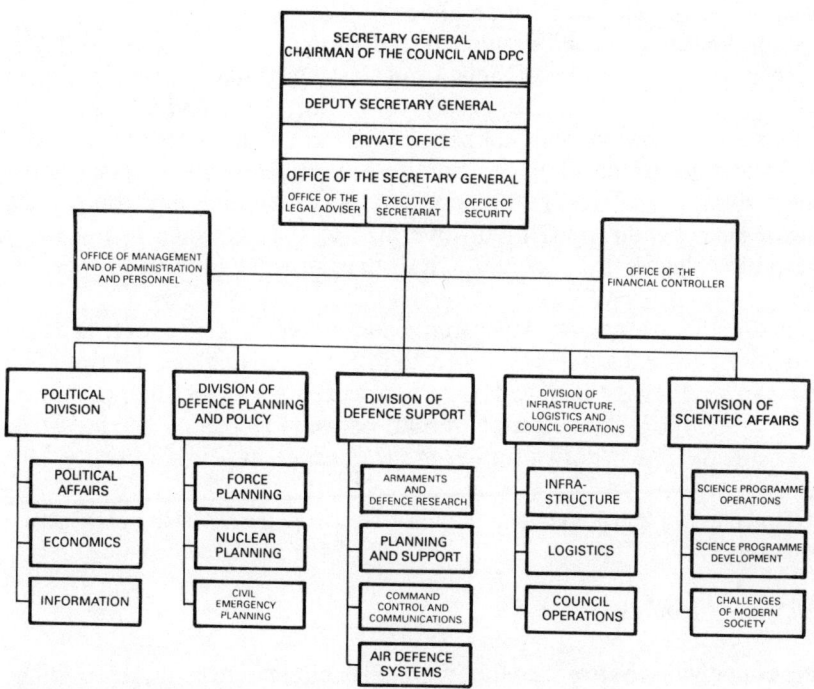

Figure 4 The formal structure of the NATO IS
Source: NATO *Facts and Figures*, 1984, p. 92

'Political Division' and 'Division of Defence Planning and Policy' (see Figure 4) are those two out of the five Divisions that the Secretary General is able to lead best (i 14, i 43). 'Division of Infrastructure etc.' is in a middle position, whereas 'Division of Defence Support'[20] is clearly at the bottom (i 14, i 30). The Division 'does not want guidance from above' (i 14), and is dominated by a 'we know best attitude' (i 14). Part of the reason for this state of affairs is indicated to be the (lack of) willingness to cooperate on the part of the shifting ASGs for the Division (i 14, i 30). To this should be added, however, that the field is more difficult to routinize and establish in a certain pattern than Defence Planning or Infrastructure (see the relevant chapters in Part III). The field is also internally difficult to coordinate, among other things because there are much too few IS civil servants to 'cover' the very large number of committees and sub-committees within the field.

These observations all pertain to the (lack of) possibilities to lead the Staff Divisions. It is replied from the Leadership that it is not *necessary* to lead all Divisions equally tight (i 28). The most 'technical' ones should be allowed to be rather self-contained, generally speaking. But *when* issues of top-level interest have knocked on the door of a technical field like infrastructure (the freezing of contributions from a certain member country, the Greek/Turkish relationship), guidance has been possible.[21]

Turning, finally, to the *willingness* to lead, it is not as self-evident as it may sound, from an *a priori* point of view. Lord Carrington has been praised from all sides (the IS, delegations, Ministries) for his interest in and efforts for the Staff. This effort, however, has not been enough to compensate for the sins of previous times, given his relatively short time in office. His predecessors have displayed a varying interest in the Staff and its functioning; in certain cases, they have been handicapped by an intermediate layer, which has actually sought to block leadership: 'there is a Staff to ensure that nothing happens' (i 14).

Taken together, we can say that not only does the actual degree of leadership seem to vary between Divisions: it is also rather weak in general terms. The main reason for this may very well be the lack of a career service that was noted previously (and the lack of rotation of Staff between Divisions, see p. 57). In an interview, the line is drawn further to the question of self-control:

> There is boundary defence and sets of blinkers between the Divisions; nations take advantage of that (i 14).

Bureaucratic Ideology

Another conceivable bulwark against national encirclement could be a particular bureaucratic ideology prevailing in the ICS in question (Downs, 1967, p. 237).

> a verbal image of that portion of the good society relevant to the functions of the particular bureau concerned, plus the chief means of constructing that portion.

A bureaucratic ideology can be useful for the ICS both externally (see pp. 19, 105–21) and, as we shall see here, internally. It may be induced consciously from the ICS leadership, as part of an attempt to improve hierarchical control. Also, however, it may exist 'spontaneously', that is, without any conscious inducement. This may be the case with a certain professional *esprit de corps*, based on the employees' common educational background, as one can imagine (for example, in WMO). Where such common background is lacking, there may be more macro-oriented ideologies available, like an amorphous 'European' ideology in the EC Commission.

It seems obvious that the stronger the bureaucratic ideology, the more a kind of 'we feeling' will prevail in the ICS that may serve, *ceteris paribus*, as a certain bulwark against external pressure (proposition 5, Figure 3). A good example of this is provided by Ascher (1983, p. 437):

> In one important respect the World Bank differs from certain other international agencies in which the problem of national identification and rivalry creates a high level of conflict and debate. Because of the cosmopolitan training of top economists and engineers, the personnel in professional positions in the World Bank behave very much alike, whether they be Indian, English, Argentine, or Canadian. The World Bank mirrors the ideological divisions of the international 'developmental community'. Thus the ideological division within the Bank is not a conflict between North and South as much as between the Chicago School and the Sussex School.

A certain professional *esprit de corps*, hence, is believed to increase the ICS internationalism (self-control).

I believe, though, that the material and palpable foundation for a 'we feeling' may be the existence of a career service, as analysed above. This provides individual civil servants with a sense of 'common fate' that will be absent in a system of fixed-term appointments, for natural reasons. Apart from this, the sheer time available for an 'indoctrination' in a bureau ideology, be it from above or from colleagues, will be insufficient in the latter case (see also Bennett, 1988, p. 391). So if there is no career service, it is seen here as rather marginal what a bureaucratic ideology can accomplish.

NATO: Bureaucratic ideology The macro-ideology that almost presents itself regarding the NATO IS is Western democratic pluralism, perhaps supplemented with a marked anti-Communist world view. This can be deduced from NATO's purposes, described in its Charter. There is no empirical evidence available, however, showing that NATO civil servants should be more ideologically motivated as described above than other civil servants. One can have a vague, intuitive feeling that this is the case, but it is hard to see, which empirical technique, if any, should display such a tendency satisfactorily. We must rest content with observing that the ideology is 'available', in view of the official purposes of the Alliance.

The question remains if there exists any lower-level bureaucratic ideology leading to a certain 'we feeling'. It turns out that the *esprit de corps* is markedly weaker than in a national administration. Apart from the heterogeneity that will always characterize an ICS, it should be emphasized here that the civil servants have very different educational and professional backgrounds (economists, political scientists, engineers, retired military officers, and so on). The absence of a career service has already been stressed; to this could be added the multitude of different employment contracts that exist, something that does not further any particular feeling of 'being in the same boat'. The interviews that have been carried out on this question display unambiguously a relatively weak *esprit de corps* in the NATO IS.[22]

Reachability: Generally and in NATO

This factor refers to the availability of good communication channels between the ICS and member governments. The best communication channels exist, when governments regard the IO as so important that they establish delegations (embassies) attached to the IO/ICS Headquarters. The larger the delegations, the better and more nuanced communication possibilities. A further factor are the technical communication facilities, both between delegations and their respective capitals and between delegations and the ICS.

High reachability bears with it both advantages and disadvantages, from the viewpoint of the ICS. As to the latter, it is obvious that more national civil servants physically on the spot increases the risk of the ICS being penetrated. There is a greater risk that the individual ICS civil servant is nationally encircled. Hence, the ICS self-control is reduced (proposition 7a). The direct effect from reachability on influence capability is harder to tell (7b, see Figure 3). It seems that we must here distinguish between ICSs that have a crucial implementation role of their own (and hence a certain prior influence) and those that do not. Regarding the former, the ICS influence capability (and autonomy) will be reduced by the presence of a large number of national civil servants watching their activities. National control with the ICS (see the Introduction) will be increased (that is, in general, not only between fellow countrymen). As to the latter case, with little ICS influence, the ICS can probably improve its modest influence, the more national civil servants that are close at hand. The ICS avoids becoming a desert island that no crucial clients are interested in.[23]

It should be mentioned here that there are differences between issue areas in this question; delegations cover all the IO activities, but they do make priorities, evidently, between various areas of an IO's activities. The risk of encirclement, hence, differs between areas, as we shall see in Part III.

As already mentioned, governments have relatively large delegations at the NATO HQ in Brussels. Vandevanter (1970, p. 106) stresses in his comparison of the roles of the Secretary-General and SACEUR that

> ...it seems, paradoxically, that the proximity of the Secretary General to the decision makers has handicapped him... . Sitting so close to the Council members, and having them readily available for consultation, he is obliged to clear even minor matters with them before issuing instructions.

There is every reason to believe that this observation is valid analogously for civil servants at lower levels in relation to their committee colleagues from the delegations. Hence, this should be an illustration of proposition (7b).

The NATO International Staff Internationalism

One set of the propositions that have been argued above have all the ICS self-control (internationalism) as their dependent variable. We have so far classified the NATO IS according to the various independent variables. It remains to analyse the NATO IS internationalism, that is, the dependency homewards for individual NATO civil servants. This is a much more difficult task, because 'instructions' from any authority other than NATO is against the NATO Staff Rules (art. 2, 1 July 1955) that has been modelled after the UN Staff Regulation previously cited (p. 36).

What can be said with certainty on the basis of interviews is that delegation civil servants use their nationals in the IS to get information about issues that are 'under way' (i 2) ('early warning' (i 27)), and about the attitudes of other delegations in certain matters; conversely, the IS civil servants get information on what will be acceptable to the delegation. On top of all this comes, of course, general gossip in both directions, and one can always give each other a 'helping hand' (i 1) in both practical and substantial matters.

A couple of examples could be offered: the Ambassador of country X calls his national in the Secretary General's Private Office and gets news about other delegations' attitudes in a certain matter, or rumours of initiatives under way. Or the Defence Counsellor in delegation Y calls his national in the Infrastructure Directorate in order to disentangle a complicated NATO-funded construction matter in country Y in an 'adroit' and flexible way (i 33), even if it is a civil servant of nationality Z, who stands for the inspection of the construction.

It is common practice not to bypass the civil servant handling a specific case (i 3). But that does not exclude that one contacts a national in the same section or directorate. The communication advantages springing from the community of language, culture, and so on cannot be discounted. In that witches' cauldron of different languages and circus language that an ICS constitutes, the advantage of expressing oneself in one's own language can hardly be overestimated (i 20), thereby avoiding the numerous misunderstandings that the language barrier carries with it, even for the language skilled.

Also, the physical facilities are emphasized in interviews (for example, i 2): firstly that the IS and delegations are located in the same building in a common HQ and, secondly, the non-trivial fact that they have common cafeteria. This absolutely furthers the information communication, not least between fellow countrymen in the IS and delegations.

Generally speaking, the Great Powers are said to be those in closest contact with their NATO nationals (i 1). For the US, there exists a special dependency homewards in view of their employment's national career value, among other things (i 5).[24] It is said about the Germans in the ICS, semi-jokingly, that they communicate more closely with Bonn than even the German delegation does (i 5).[25]

In what has been said, so far, however, there is nothing that necessarily implies a lack of IS self-control. If contacts develop to pressure or outright instructions, as are well-documented from other IOs (see pp. 35–7), is, of course, difficult to reveal:

- Lobbyism and perhaps even outright pressure may occur; more for some than for others. (i 2)

- We are the 'nice guys'; others are much worse. The Great Powers generally employ people that are 'reliable'. (i 6)

- Delegations are internationalized, and the IS is sometimes nationalized; there is no pattern, though. Some IS people are actively seeking instructions. (i 35)

These are the strongest statements that have been made (i 2 and i 35 in delegations, i 6 in the IS). There have been no counter-statements, denying that external instruction should sometimes take place. Statements of the type 'the other ones are the bad guys' can hardly be ascribed much source value, when taken at face value (see below though).

It is probably beyond doubt that pressure is sometimes exerted, mostly by the Great Powers on their nationals. It is hard to believe, though, that NATO civil servants should be instructed to further specific *initiatives* from their countries. The fact that nationals are not placed hierarchically over each other, and that national quotas apply also at section level, makes it difficult to imagine that a country should be able to lobby initiatives through the IS (i 19). The 'pressure' or 'instructions' mentioned in interviews must refer to a kind of (weakened) veto-power, that is, that governments can stop, weaken or retard 'unfortunate' initiatives at their very birth, by virtue of their connections in the IS.

We should return to 'the other ones are the bad guys' syndrome; this exists for sure. And it has a life of its own, quite independently of the actual 'badness' taking place. This means that the IS and its salient environment has obviously entered the vicious circle, where mutual suspicion is prevailing, and where individual governments, to be on the safe side, in order not to be superseded by the 'bad' ones, feel it necessary to influence 'their' people in a direction that can hinder or weaken certain initiatives.

Conclusion: How Can ICS Internationalism be Improved, and What has NATO Done?

If we sum up the factors that should be manipulated if one wishes to strengthen ICSs' self-control (internationalism) we should emphasize the following ones: the principle of merit should be applied in connection with appointments and promotions (versus national quotas), and a career service should be established.

Apart from its own contributions to ICS self-control, it would also indirectly support it through the factors of leadership and bureaucratic ideology. It is not believed that the latter would have any significant impact, without the existence of a career service. Regarding the factors of national career value and reachability, we remember that a favourable effect from them upon ICS self-control (see Figure 3) would have some effects on the ICS influence capability that would probably not be desirable. So it seems obvious that the factor that should be done something about, primarily, is the one pertaining to career service, with the principle of merit in second place.

These measures, it should be remembered, are those that should be taken on the basis of the pure counterweight conception, saying that strengthened ICSs should be established as (modest) counterweights to nation states and their governments. If we sum up what NATO has done in the relevant respects, it amounts to the following: in the two crucial respects, NATO has *not* followed the counterweight conception; there is no career service, and the principle of merit is only applied within narrow constraints set by national quotas. In these respects, NATO has followed the resignist conception of the ICS, acquiescing in governments' reluctance to give up control. Without a career service, there is not much *esprit de corps* in the IS (also due, though, to other factors). Regarding type of leadership, however, one can say that NATO has followed the counterweight conception through its unitary leadership, a Secretary General. But the latter's willingness, or possibilities, to lead the Staff has not always been present. Taken together, we can say that the NATO IS is obviously based on a resignist conception.

In spite of the sensitivity of the issue, it was found that IS civil servants face a problem of dependency homewards, though varying with nationality and other factors. Hence, the NATO IS forms no exception to those other ICSs, whose problems of self-control have been noted in the literature. We cannot, of course, indicate any critical threshold, saying that the IS self-control is 'too low'. But it is certain that a vicious circle exists, with mutual suspicions regarding 'instructions'. And this limits creativity and influence capability, irrespective of the *actual* extent of instructions.

Should NATO Have Done Differently?

Should NATO have used a different staffing policy for its IS, then? In the light of the previous section, the answer to this question may seem obvious. However, it is not that simple. It could be argued that even if proposition (1) (see p. 38) is valid generally, it does not apply in a NATO context. Here, the problem of internationalism is not an important problem, in the first place. There are also a range of special circumstances about NATO that might make our arguments irrelevant. There could be side-effects of the suggested measures that we have not dealt with. This will be discussed in the present section.

We shall first look at some often-heard reasons for NATO's present staffing policy, stressed by NATO itself, national civil servants, or external analysts. Against a career service, and in favour of national secondments to the NATO IS, the following is argued:

1. The ICS inertia is reduced; the seconded personnel admits innovative thinking from outside, and it is prevented that civil servants 'take root'. It is this way of thinking that is represented by Cox (1973, p. 167):

   The very factors which are supposed to strengthen the international character of the staff – long-term tenure of appointment, judicially interpreted administrative regulations, etc. – reinforce this *immobilisme*.

   See also Simay (1978, p. 114) in this respect.
2. The national civil services get in touch with NATO, as the seconded personnel returns home and 'sells' Alliance policy.[26]
3. The seconded civil servants improve NATO's opportunities for understanding the backgrounds of member-countries' policies, and hence also for influencing them and perhaps harmonizing them.[27]

What is common to the three arguments is the belief that self-control is not of value to the IO/ICS in the first place, or that it has so negative side-effects on influence capability that it is nothing to strive for, seen from an aggregate point of view. We shall now comment upon each of the three arguments in a NATO context.

For the purpose described in (3), one has already the national delegations at NATO HQ, even relatively large delegations with excellent communication facilities. The present system of secondment implies a kind of *double delegation system*, where nations in some cases actually have *two* sets of personnel stationed at NATO HQ.

Argument (2) does not hold water. As was pointed out (p. 47) the Foreign Services with a generalist staff policy do not use their home-coming IS employees within their field of expertise. And moreover one has, again, the delegations to safeguard this purpose. Often, delegation people are 'internationalized' (i 35) during their stays at NATO, and may therefore 'sell' Alliance policy upon returning home.

Argument (1) is the best one. Inertia seems to be a faithful companion to any type of administration in larger organizations. But why is it, one might ask, only in weak institutions like ICSs that it must be fought so eagerly? Is there not a risk of people 'taking roots' in a national ministry? In particular, in those ministries (typically the Foreign Services) that have a policy of no external input at any level, except for the bottom (that is, where one should almost start as a volunteer in order to have a career in the first place)? In that very exposed milieu that ICSs are located, surrounded by the world's strongest actors with national ministries as their spearheads, it seems that simple counterweight must have highest priority. The relatively 'harsh' means that this may, of course, have certain negative side-effects. But in this connection, there is reason to repeat the very essential and positive counterpart to inertia, namely the much improved continuity and memory that the ICS acquires by establishing a career service.[28]

In order to compensate for the inertia effect, one could also imagine that a rotation system was established among the directorates, as an integral part of the IS career service. As a matter of fact, this might actually improve the 'inertia situation' of today, where one often hears complaints (i 14, i 30) on the creation of sub-empires within the IS (see the citation on p. 50).[29] So the net sum of the measures proposed might actually be a *reduction* in inertia, not a worsening. Finally, the civil servants could, like their colleagues in the EC Commission, be sent on regular in-service training (i 12).

Taken together, it seems that the three arguments discussed above mostly have been advocated as a kind of rationalization of *status quo*, in the recognition that member governments would never allow a revision. One tries then to make a deed out of necessity by convincing oneself and others that the *status quo* is, in fact, the optimal situation.

Turning to the second major reform suggestion, the abolishing of quotas, one could also here think of negative side-effects. Not even the classical authors are, like the counterweight conception, willing to abandon all forms of quotas. Merit shall be the prime criterion of appointment, but all states shall be safeguarded a 'fair representation'. Even though it is sometimes denied, it is obvious that we face two conflicting considerations (see p. 42). Here we can see most clearly that the classical conception is no ideal type, but a practical–political construction that has made certain compromises. The classics' main arguments refer to the IO's ability to operate in relation to certain regions in the world, and to every culture's 'definite qualities of its own'[30] that the ICS could benefit from. A certain consideration for these two arguments should be easy to integrate with the principle of merit. If a position in the ICS implies contacts with a certain region, then a special knowledge of this region must, evidently, be part of the job description and hence the required merits. One might think of further regionalistic softenings; the crucial point is that they are always, in rhetoric, argued by pointing to the principle of merit. A pep-talk, once in a while, from the Secretary-General (like that of Pérez De Cuellar, 1988), would be a contribution to the bulwark against the insistence on quotas.

An objection to the abandoning of quotas says that it would favour the applications from certain countries, not least the British (for linguistic reasons, among other things) (i 3).[31] This is probably true. But it could be said here, firstly, that the simultaneous introduction of a career service will reduce the risk of nations exploiting their nationals in the IS, as previously argued. Secondly, regarding the British in particular, it should be mentioned that they, already today, often function as mediators in various committees, be they delegation or

IS civil servants. They are tailored to this purpose for linguistic reasons,[32] and they are also substantially well-suited to being Atlantic harmonizers (see p. 27) in view of their Euro–Anglo-Saxon background. So an increase in the number of British can hardly be seen as a disadvantage; quite to the contrary.[33]

One could think of situations, where the career principle and the principle of merit are in conflict. Should one, for instance, exclusively fill the top vacancies in an administration through internal recruitment, even when one knows that more qualified people can be found externally? The counterweight conception, giving top priority to institutional strengthening, would here advocate internal recruitment, because it gives the ICS a monopoly, and would be beneficial to civil servants' loyalty and motivation. The classics have, at this point, a modified attitude. There should, as mentioned by Loveday (1956, p. 102), be a 'flow of new blood', not only regarding hirings for short-term special tasks, but also as regards top posts.

In a NATO context, one should probably adhere to the classics, among other things in order to meet the inertia criticism mentioned above.[34] One could imagine an external recruitment at the ASG level. But it is important that this is only a *possibility*, in order to avoid demoralization in the IS itself. By using the principle of merit at this level it is obvious that previous service in the IS must be ascribed a considerable weight.

To conclude so far, we have, in the present section, rejected a range of assumed negative side-effects from the counterweight conception in a NATO context. When this is combined with the conception's obvious advantages for the ICS self-control and its influence capability, it should be concluded that the counterweight conception is superior to the resignist conception, also in a NATO framework. It should be repeated, though, that one could imagine a minor modification of the conception, when it comes to the possibility of external recruitment for certain top-posts. Furthermore, the principle of merit should in practice, not in rhetoric, be interpreted in a flexible way.

The fourth conception of the ICS, the *utopian* one, will only be briefly commented upon here, as it in practice pertains to a UN framework. However, the fact that utopianism constitutes an ideal type makes it well-suited to provoke discussion of some basic principles of the counterweight conception and the NATO reforms that have been suggested.

Weiss (1975, 1982) agrees with the counterweight conception in being against national influence on appointments and national quotas regarding the number of civil servants (quotas based on sex, race, age or language should be allowed). In other words: the national encirclement of the ICSs must cease. But this should not happen by establishing a counterweight in the form of a career service, and so on. There is a risk, then, that the ICS will be dominated by too much inertia and too much unengaged 'deadwood'. The international civil servants should not be attracted with tenure and large material benefits,[35] but they should instead be inspired by an engagement in the very issues at stake.

The ICS should be of modest size, decentralized (non-hierarchical), and work on an *ad hoc* basis with singular projects.

Even though the conception sounds sympathetic, and would surely be well-suited in certain other contexts, I have labelled it 'utopian', because it seems to presuppose a power vacuum in international cooperation. To believe that engagement and enthusiasm in themselves should be bulwarks against national encirclement sounds over-optimistic. Perhaps, it could work at the beginning, but it is not an unfamiliar experience that the ambitions of nation states and other strong institutions are much more persistent phenomena than individuals' engagement and enthusiasm. What happens, when the first disappointments and frustrations are met in dealings with clients, that is, not least the heavy, national bureaucracies? Would it not, then, be more tempting to return home to more stable conditions and a more stable income than the ICS can offer? The risk is, then, that projects are not completed: continuity must, in other words, become a major problem for this type of ICS.

It might perhaps be replied here that what we are actually quarrelling about is our conception of civil servants (or human beings, for that matter) at the most fundamental level, and that the counterweight conception presupposes a unilaterally materialist view that does not leave space for engagement and moral qualities.[36] The answer to this is that the utopianist, then, does not allow the conception to apply *universally*, or at least to all civil servants. Those in the career service are believed to become disengaged deadwood, because they have been over-privileged. Here, apparently, an opposite civil servant conception is prevailing. One could, of course, reply here that there exists two dichotomic types of civil servants – the 'materialists' and the 'enthusiasts' – who are attracted by each type of ICS. But even if this should be true, one may ask, as above, will not materialism come sneaking in on the enthusiasts, at least after a certain time? And one might wonder, will not enthusiasts also be attracted to a career service? Weiss' arguments pertaining to the career service can be countered on purely 'materialist' premises. Weiss is indisputably right that there exists deadwood in ICSs, as many sources indicate; but this might to a very large extent be due to the national quotas and the *lack* of a true career service. In such a service, the opportunities for promotion will be a crucial incentive that will reduce (though probably never eliminate) the problems of deadwood.[37]

Could NATO Have Done Differently?

In the previous section, I have argued against the utopian conception of the ICS. It was argued that NATO's staffing policy should have been based on the counterweight conception (with certain marginal modifications), instead of the resignist conception. But the question then is, *could* NATO have done this? The key to reform lies, of course, with member states. Even though only staffing procedure is at stake, and not the slightest traces of supranationalism are involved,[38] states have been reluctant. As expressed by an interviewee from a small state delegation (who saw a stronger ICS as an advantage for small states):

> States will not allow a stronger ICS. (i 8, also i 1, i 4, i 7)

The same, slightly cryptic, formulation is often heard. The reason *why* is never really spelled out,[39] but will be subject to speculation here. One thing is to abstain from a range of collective advantages that have been pointed out above: to have the ICS as a creative initiator, conflict preventor and active mediator in connection with member disagreements (that have been frequent during the 1980s, see p. 27). To safeguard a reasonable continuity in ICS work, and to be able to hire the most competent civil servants. This abstention from a range of collective advantages may, however, be understood (though not applauded), if the attitudes are based on substantial, though narrow, national interests, as these are perceived. But such are hardly involved, as it seems.

We have observed the eagerness of governments in trying to acquire posts to their nationals in the NATO IS. This contrasts with the fact that some countries have obvious difficulties in filling their quota with competent people, whilst others use NATO or other ICSs as a kind of 'dumping ground' for people, they for one reason or the other wish to get rid of. Of course, there are certain advantages as to communication to have many nations in the IS, and they may, at best, be able to 'veto' unfortunate proposals from their very start. But one should ask, if this is not a rather redundant security obsession, given the fact that governments have influence and veto power in the committee work, and in the many informal talks with representatives of other delegations?

For lack of satisfactory substantial explanations for states' reluctance to strengthen ICSs, one here gets the suspicion that we are dealing with a self-reinforcing competition between governments (notably their Foreign Services), the purpose of which is to win the most posts at the best levels, only because this is something that can be easily quantified and compared (an indicator of diplomatic skill). The suspicion, hence, is that we are dealing with narrow-minded prestige, and security obsession, rather than narrow-minded substance, and departmental interests rather than national interests.

Uncertainty Avoidance

As Part II has had a prescriptive aim, that is, the suggestion of reform, we have focused on explanatory factors that can be the subject of manipulation. We should finish by some general comments on the potential 'manipulators', that is, the ICS's authority actors: nation states and their governments. It was said at the outset that they are, indisputably, the world's strongest actors. State leaders' rhetoric on the desirability of 'fruitful international cooperation' should lead one to believe that they would not use their power and influence to counteract the existence of creative and influential international institutions that could further such cooperation. This is, however, what they do, not only as regards NATO. If we generalize the explanation that was given in the previous section, pertaining to NATO, we come to the factor of 'uncertainty avoidance', that is, that governments are excessively obsessed with avoiding uncertainty, also sometimes at the price of substantial benefits. This factor will be treated in its proper context in Part III (pp. 72–73); suffice it to emphasize here that uncertainty avoidance on the part of IO member governments seems to be the major explanation for nation states hindering the emergence of crucial instruments of fruitful international cooperation. It may well be, as the NATO (and other) examples bear witness, that in particular the Great Powers are 'responsible' here; we then get a self-reinforcing mechanism so that *all* governments must safeguard their 'interests', so as not to lag behind the others. These self-reinforcing mechanisms, combined with uncertainty avoidance on the part of governments, are probably the main underlying explanations for the ICSs' lack of internationalism.[40]

Notes – Part II

1. Some of the underlying causes for this control problem are expressed by Downs (1967) in the following way:

   Each official tends to distort the information he passes upwards in the hierarchy, exaggerating those data favourable to himself and minimizing those unfavourable to himself.   (p. 266, see also chapter VII)

   In a bureau hierarchy, information passed upward to the topmost official tends to be distorted so as to more closely reflect what he would like to hear, or his preconceived views, than reality warrants.   (p. 269, see also chapter X)

   Each official will vary the degree to which he complies with directives from his superiors, depending upon whether those directives favor or oppose his own interests.
   (p. 266, see also chapter VII)

   These mechanisms are likely to be somewhat 'counterbiased' at the top, but not adequately to avoid distortion. For some developments of this way of thinking, see Larsen (1986), further stressing the impossibility of top-level control. See also Lundqvist (1987) chapter 7.1.

2. As witnessed by Soviet dissidents (for example, Shevchenko), Soviet nationals serving in the UN Secretariat were normally expected to act as spies for their country and were bound by instructions from home (Reymond and Mailick, 1986, p. 138). Such are, of course, the most extreme examples of dependency homewards for individual civil servants. However,

62 *The International Civil Service*

with the changed Soviet view of the UN in current years, there are signs also of a changed view of the very concept of the ICS (See Note 14).

3. Since the McCarthy era, the USA has a special system for securing that its nationals serving as IGO civil servants remain loyal to – the United States! (Weiss, 1982, pp. 294–297; Jacobson, 1984, p. 91). This implies that US applicants are scrutinized by a US Commission, whose veto it is hoped that the ICS in question will follow. Since 1975 though, the procedure has been somewhat more relaxed.

   Also, clearances of their nationals are sometimes made by other governments. If an ICS is willing, without further questions, to fire one of its employees upon a negative national clearing outcome, then its self-control is, evidently, highly questionable (i 34).

4. An example of (completely unfounded) mutual suspicion and its effects could be the fate of the very competent French ASG for Economic and Financial Affairs, Didier Gregh (1955–1967). As analysed by Jordan (1979, pp. 123–124):

   In general, Stikker [The Secretary-General] did not enjoy working with the French, because he felt they were constantly raising objections and creating tensions. But Gregh, who maintained good relationships with Quai d'Orsay, was able to retain Stikker's confidence. Unfortunately, his nationality made his position conditional in the eyes of the Americans... when the French and the British quarreled over British membership in the EEC, Gregh suffered on two fronts. He lost whatever standing he had with the Gaullists because of his good working relations with the British, who in turn shied away from dealing with him because of the coolness and suspicion French Gaullism had engendered in NATO.

   On governments' uncertainty avoidance, see pp. 60–1. The loser in government clashes always seems to be the ICS and its individual civil servants.

5. Obviously, also the twin category of ICS autonomy is involved here. Member governments having 'Trojan horses' within the ICS entails, evidently, that the ICS becomes more vulnerable to pressure. And not only pressure that is led through these channels of instrumentality, but also other types of pressure, as the ICS general image and respect among governments is weakened. Autonomy is, however, so closely related to influence capability that we have not given it independent consideration here. Our main concern is, evidently, what happens to the ability to exert influence.

6. Of course, actors other than ICSs may further international cooperation through, for example, a bridge-building effort. But as was argued on pp. 24–5, the ICSs are likely to be particularly well-suited to this role.

7. For a survey of the 'classics', see Weiss (1975, chapter 2) or Weiss (1982). See also the memoire literature that I referred to in the Introduction. On the British roots of the classical ICS conception, see Jordan (1971b). As already mentioned, the first practical inspiration for this conception was the secretariat of the League of Nations.

8. The classical conception is also, evidently, a rather amorphous one, being a construction on the basis of several authors, each of them having special practical experiences.

9. As formulated by Reymond and Mailick (1986, p. 139):

   And here, as in Gresham's law, the bad may drive out the good. Governments that are faithful to the principles of the Charter may often be pushed to follow the examples of others so as not to let them solely influence the staffing operations.

10. As with proposition (1), the most ambitious roles are those that will suffer; perhaps also the expert role due to less competent civil servants.

11. As shown by the UN history, there are numerous conceptions of this (Damsgaard, 1983, p. 114): states' contributions to the common budget, their population sizes, or a range of weighted criteria.

12. Regarding this and the following propositions, the NATO IS will serve as an illustration of the relevant independent variable. For a survey of the NATO institutional structure, see pp. 6–8.
13. Of which one that should not be underestimated is the family advantage (that is, the partner's career opportunities, the children's schooling, and so on)
14. It should be mentioned here also that certain UN member countries, notably the Eastern Bloc, did not allow their nationals, until recently, an ICS career. In accordance with their traditional view of the ICS concept, they practised a system of stationing civil servants for fixed-term periods (Morawiecki, 1968). However, there are tendencies at present, with the changed Soviet view of the UN at the general level, for the Soviets to allow some of their nationals a UN career (de Cuellar, 1988, p. 95; Jonah, 1988, p. 104).
15. Understood simply as the value that the international service is expected to have for a future national career, both specifically regarding promotion opportunities, but also as regards 'reputation' in broader terms.
16. To be a bit source critical here, all these interviewees were national civil servants. It is always tempting, of course, to ascribe a relatively low reputation to a neighbouring category of civil servants. However, the international civil servants being recruited from national (Foreign) Services, to a large extent, makes their reputation here a crucial factor, even if one may feel it unfair.
17. The relatively short average employment periods in the NATO IS imply that the personal contact net in Brussels of a former NATO civil servant will quickly melt away (i 1). So if his NATO experience, at least in this regard, shall be of any use, it should probably be right away upon his return from Brussels.
18. The situation appears to be no better for other ICSs than NATO, for example, the EC Commission. It seems, though, that the situation has been improving slightly in current years, as there exist a few examples where ICS posts (preferably as Chiefs of Cabinet) have led to career promotion at home (or at least not inhibited it). In these cases, however, it has often been necessary to safeguard this promotion at the highest levels (the Foreign Minister or the Director of the Foreign Ministry) (i 43). This, in itself, bears witness of the 'out of sight, out of mind' problem.
19. This is a general US personnel policy *vis-à-vis* IOs. Modelski (1970, p. 210) analyses the SEATO international civil servants, employed at its Headquarter in Bangkok:

    Their outlook is molded by the national service which in due course they expect to re-enter, and their careers are unlikely to be greatly influenced by the quality of their performance at SEATO.... In certain national services – for example, the United States Foreign Service – an officer's work is annually reported upon by his embassy and forms part of his career record; this procedure helps to uphold higher work standards, but it militates against the growth of SEATO loyalties.

    This is in fine harmony with propositions (6a) and (6b).
20. As to the nature of the field, see in Figure 4 the names of the various directorates under the 'Division of Defence Support'. As to defence planning and infrastructure, see the relevant chapters in Part III.
21. Whether this attitude is a kind of rationalization, given the actual possibilities of leadership, is, of course, another question that it is hardly possible to answer.
22. This conclusion is based on five mutually independent interview statements (i 4, i 6, i 7, i 8, i 10) (none in the opposite direction). There is a fine spreading: one former employee, one delegation civil servant and three present employees (of which two at the level of Chiefs).
23. Regarding the ICS influence capability, the size of the ICS itself is, evidently, also crucial. In the former case, with a crucial ICS implementation responsibility, its influence will be improved, the better the *ratio* between ICS civil servants and national civil servants (sum

of delegation staffs). In the latter case, one could probably say that ICS influence increases with the *sum* of ICS and delegation civil servants together.

24. The interviews made by Beer (1969) concerning dependency homewards for SHAPE officers seem to indicate that the USA is the country holding its people in the tightest grip:

> ...the United States puts a pretty tight curb on its people but other countries do it much less (interview in a European delegation to NATO HQ, pp. 194–5).

This accords with my own interviews (i 5, i 21, i 23). One cannot obviously make uncritical inferences from SHAPE to the IS. But it seems to be a fact that governments' 'policies' *vis-à-vis* their nationals in international service are general, that is, cover all IOs. On the US attitude to Americans in SEATO, see Note 19. See also the section on national career value of international service, p. 46, and Note 25.

25. If we retain the assumption of generality from the previous note, the following observations are of interest. Scheinman (1971, p. 206) describes contacts homewards for EC commissioners:

> Fairly close contact is maintained with the home bureaucracy for the most part although this is more true for nationals of some states (France, West Germany and Italy) than for those of others (the Netherlands and Belgium).

A distinction between Small Powers and Great Powers seems, apparently, also to be relevant here. The explanation is probably the Great Powers' larger resources for analysis. In other words, they are able to form an opinion also on relatively detailed questions. This is in fine accordance with Jacobson's (1974) observation that the US and the Soviet Union are those Powers in the United Nations that supply their delegations with the most rigid instructions (pp. 101–103). It is close at hand to believe that this tendency also applies regarding their *international* civil servants (in a weakened version, of course).

26. As already expressed by Lord Ismay (1954, p. 64):

> ...it ensures that member governments have in their service an increasing number of officers with special knowledge of NATO affairs.

See also Jacobson (1984, p. 90).

27. See James (1971, p. 67) – even though referring to a UN context.

28. Having considered arguments for and against regarding job security, James (1971, p. 70) concludes:

> All that can be said is that the UN experience tends to demonstrate that the disadvantages of job security are more than compensated for by the advantages.

29. There is no rotation system today, the reason being that people are hired for so relatively short periods anyway that there is no point in rotating them.
30. Ranshofen-Wertheimer (1945) p. 352, cited from Damsgaard (1983), p. 33.
31. The USA has, on the whole, the best qualified potential appliers (see p. 47). But for purely geographical reasons, the 'risk' of an American invasion would be very limited. The USA is actually, at present, 'underrepresented' in the IS, and has always been (at least to my knowledge).
32. It may sound trivial but should be emphasized, still: if both participants in a negotiation speak their second language, the communication is significantly weakened compared with the situation where one of them (here the British) speaks his or her native language.

33. Also, one should expect more Dutch and Belgians in the Staff than at present, due to the geographical proximity and their relatively high level of education. Apart from the decreased importance of nationalities in a career service, in the first place, it is hard to see anything unfortunate in such a development, Holland and Belgium being small states in the Alliance.
34. According to Downs (1967, p. 275 and chapter XVI),

    The rate at which innovation will be suggested by bureau members will be greater... the greater the degree to which it fills high-level vacancies with 'outsiders' rather than by promoting from within.

35. The consequences of 'excessive personal enrichment' in an ICS and its delegations are also argued by Ramsay (1984), pertaining to UNCTAD.
36. See our assumptions p. 12, from Downs (1967).
37. To meet Weiss' and Ramsay's criticism a little bit on the way, one could imagine ICS fringe benefits being reduced, in return for the introduction of a career service.
38. In contrast to Hartley (1963), who suggested a reform in the direction of supranationality, inspired by the EC Commission.
39. Not due to secrecy, I believe, but simply because there seems to be no sensible reason; see below.
40. One should believe, *a priori*, uncertainty avoidance to be strongest in connection with highly heterogeneous IOs, where the ground is fertile in advance for mutual suspicion. Hence, our observations and explanations regarding uncertainty avoidance in a NATO context are remarkable, given the homogeneous nature of NATO, seen in a global-comparative perspective.

Part III The Influence of the International Civil Service: Where, How and Why?

Introduction

What has been said so far about the environment and the values of the ICS (see Part I) and the dependency of the individual civil servant *vis-à-vis* the home country (see Part II) has pertained to an IO in all of its areas of activity. Civil servant dependency does not vary systematically with issue areas (or directorates). Part I has been held at such a general level that distinctions between issue areas have been unnecessary. Here in Part III, we shall analyse the roles that are actually played by the ICS, the influence that is exerted through these, and we shall establish a general model that can explain this influence, relative to the influence of national civil servants. For this purpose, distinctions between issue areas are indispensable. As we shall see, to sum up the various (NATO) areas in an aggregate analysis would only blur significant aspects of reality; the mutual differences are too significant.[1]

Firstly, some hypotheses will be mentioned that have the influence of the ICS as their dependent variable.

Hypotheses on the Influence of the International Civil Service

That national civil services often exert influence by, for example, implementing political decisions in a different way than was intended at the top, is generally accepted in the literature on public administration.[2] The scant literature on the ICS has no unambiguous message in this regard.[3] McLaren (1980a) offers the most systematic, empirical effort to answer the question. On the basis of an investigation into a number of UN specialized agencies' ICSs, four hypotheses found support as to what determines the influence ('policy effect') of an ICS. They say, in slightly revised form (*ibid.*, p. 139):

1. The more program oriented the IO (vs. 'secretariat oriented'), the more policy-effect will be exerted by the ICS.
2. The less member governments can control the ICS civil servants, the more policy effect will be exerted by the ICS.
3. The less the technical expertise of member governments compared with that of the ICS, the more policy effect will be exerted by the ICS.
4. The more implementation carried out by the ICS, the more policy effect will it exert.

It should be added that McLaren's investigations do *not* display a policy effect from ICS activities in the preparation phase, such as preparing agenda, gathering data, identifying problems, and so on (*ibid.*, pp. 122, 138).

As 'influence' is conceived here, we are dealing with the actual *exertion* of influence, that is, the ICS's modification of other actors' behaviour in any phase of the decision-making process, through the playing of the various roles stipulated in Part I. This corresponds neatly to McLaren's 'policy effect', and should be distinguished from the concept of 'influence *capability*' (see Part I, Figure 2 and Part II, Figure 3). Therefore, McLaren's hypotheses can easily be used here. The essence of (2) above has already been dealt with in Part II. The others will be discussed here, as they will be integrated in a comprehensive model outlining the determining factors for ICS influence.

The Issue-Area Model

The model's basic factor is partly derived from McLaren's distinction between IOs that are 'programme oriented' and those that are 'secretariat oriented' (*ibid.*, pp. 10–13, 88–90, 134–7). The distinction is (mostly) inductively derived from a classification of UN specialized agencies. These are classified by McLaren in two main categories: the secretariat-oriented ones, whose primary task is the coordination between member countries, and the programme-oriented ones, whose main task is the provision of aid programmes to individual countries.[4] The former ones (*ibid.*, p. 9) have been established

> ...because, in each case, some material object is physically moved across the frontiers of some nation-states. This means that a certain amount of cooperation among these nation-states is demanded by the situation, and an international secretariat must be created to promote coordination among all the nation-states that choose to be involved.

The 'object' can be mail, electronically communicated messages, aeroplanes, ships, weather systems, and so on. Correspondingly have been established UPU (Universal Postal Union), ITU (International Telecommunication Union), ICAO (International Civil Aviation Organization), IMCO (Inter-Governmental Maritime Consultative Organization) and WMO (World Meteorological Organization).

For the programme-oriented IOs, there is not the same urgent need of coordination. The needs are located *within* individual member countries (*ibid.*, p. 11):

> Rather than strive for international cooperation *among* individual nation-states, they must develop programs *within* individual nation-states.

ILO (International Labor Organization) seeks to improve working conditions in member countries, WHO (World Health Organization) in health conditions, FAO (Food and Agricultural Organization) the state of agriculture, and so on. Evidently, these IOs require a good deal of member coordination, but it is not their primary purpose. It is to develop programmes within member countries.

It is my view that McLaren's distinction is conceptually unsatisfactory. It mixes two logically independent dimensions that each, for different reasons, contribute to a strengthening of the ICS influence. One is the needs' location, that is, the needs that the IO is officially designed to fulfil: are they located *between* IO member countries (of an inter-state nature) or *within* IO member countries (of an intra-state nature)? The other dimension pertains to the question of common programmes: does the IO and, hence, the ICS have such at its disposal, or does it not? It is McLaren's assumption that the programme-oriented IOs serve 'within needs', and that those dedicated to 'between needs' seldom have programmes. However, one should not conceptually rule out those IOs that serve 'between needs' with common programmes as a significant instrument, for example WMO (discussed by McLaren himself pp. 6–13) and NATO infrastructure (see below, pp. 89–105).

Turning to the 'issue-area model', an issue area is stipulated here simply as an area (field) of politics, characterized by the pursuit of a certain perceived need by relevant actors, be it in cooperation and/or conflict, and be it nationally, regionally, or globally delimited.[5] The concept, hence, is broader than McLaren's focus in the sense that we do not *presuppose* the existence of an IO/ICS designed for the pursuit of the need in question. However, as we are interested in the influence of ICSs, it is obvious that our focus, in practice, will not deviate much from that of McLaren.

The fundamental explanatory factor in the model will be labelled the 'basic character' of an issue area. It consists of two logically independent dimensions, one being the issue-area needs' location ('within needs' versus 'between needs'), as conceived by McLaren, the other being the 'height' of the issue area, that is, whether it belongs to high politics or low politics. This refers to national top decision-makers' view of the area: is it closely related to perceived national core values (high politics), or is it not (low politics)?[6] This is, evidently, a question of degree, and it may vary over time for an issue area. High politics areas will be followed closely by top decision-makers themselves, whereas low politics will typically be delegated to civil servants. As a useful indicator of the height of politics could be mentioned the existence of a common IO/ICS programme (budget) in the area: in low politics, top decision-makers will be willing to allow the IO/ICS a common budget, if this is seen as serving the perceived need in question, and in spite of the loss of control that it necessarily entails (see further below). Not so in high politics.[7]

Needs' Location \ The Height of Politics	Low Politics	High Politics
Within Countries	*I* Global Health (WHO)	*IV* Neutral Countries' Security (No IO)
Between Countries	*II* Global Weather Forecasts (WMO)	*III* Foreign Policy Coordination Betweeen EC Countries (EPC (within EC))

Figure 5   The four basic characters of issue areas

For each character, an issue area has been indicated as an example, and an IO (if any) in the area has been mentioned. See List of Abbreviations.

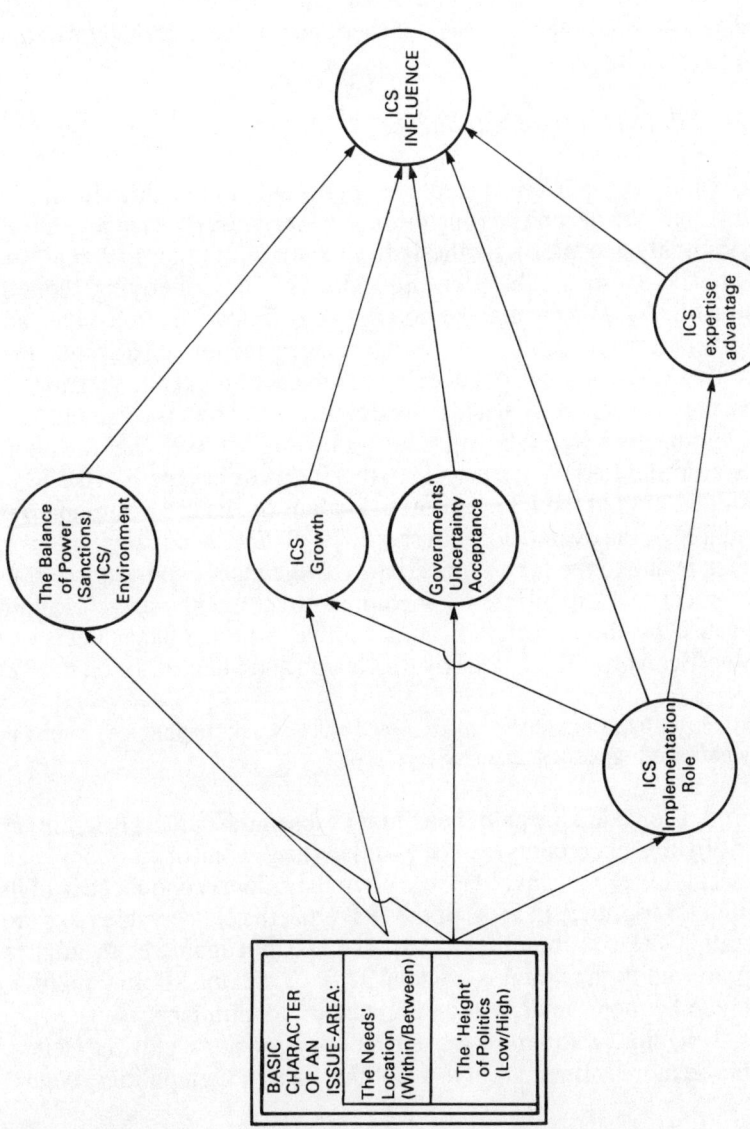

Figure 6 The basic character of an issue area determining the ICS influence in the area

Arrows indicate assumed causal relationships

It should be stressed here that the two dimensions of 'basic character' are non-reducible to underlying, more 'basic', properties of an issue area. They are, in themselves, fundamental properties of an issue area.[8] By combining the two dimensions, we get, evidently, four basic characters of issue areas (see Figure 5). We shall now see, how and why basic character of an issue area determines the relative influence of the area's ICS (if any). The reasoning that follows is illustrated in Figure 6. As should appear, the basic character is kept as one single factor (for reasons of simplicity), consisting of two mutually independent dimensions; as we shall see now, each of them determines, through different 'channels', the ICS influence.[9]

The 'Height of Politics' and ICS Influence

The height of politics and ICS influence are connected through three channels. We shall first consider the one passing through '*uncertainty acceptance*'. It is, in fact, a commonly accepted hypothesis (for example, Jönsson, 1986, p. 44) that influential ICSs are unlikely in high politics. The underlying thought mechanics of this hypothesis may be construed as follows: nation states are generally reluctant to yield autonomy to other actors, including ICSs that they have themselves originally designed, being members of the IO in question. In other words, they are generally afraid to lose control. A counter-argument here would say that this loss would be made up for by the fact that other member-states suffer a similar loss. When we add to this the presumed gain in the form of better safeguarding of the IO's substantial values by the more autonomous and influential ICS, the overall account should be obviously positive. It is not, however. This is due to the factor 'uncertainty avoidance', well-known from organization theory.[10] Organizations, including governments, strive to avoid uncertainty, also by the sacrifice of considerable benefits. Their decision-makers prefer (Schwartz, 1967, cited by McGowan and Shapiro, 1973, p. 187)

> ...alternatives with lower gains but also lower costs and risks to policies promising greater benefits at higher cost and risk levels.

In other words, a considerable gain (here, in IO substantial values) is willingly renounced, if by this uncertainty can be avoided (here, control/autonomy can be retained). This uncertainty avoidance is obviously more pronounced in high politics than in low politics. In areas of the first type, the conceivable risks are so much greater ('catastrophes'). The gains are also, but again, the avoidance of risks is preferred to the winning of gains, *ceteris paribus*. In low politics, there is likely to be more 'uncertainty acceptance', for similar reasons. From this follows, then, more willingness to yield autonomy/control to ICSs. Hence, the latter will be more influential in low politics than in high politics, *ceteris paribus*.[11]

The Influence of the International Civil Service: Where, How and Why?

To put it inversely, and in other words, in high politics, where top decision-makers are unwilling to leave matters to their own (national) civil servants, they will be even less willing to concede autonomy and influence to international civil servants.[12]

Another channel leading from the height of politics to ICS influence (see Figure 6) passes through the factors of *ICS implementation role* and ICS expertise advantage. In low politics, where we assume that national governments allow the relevant IO to have common programmes, it is not unlikely that its ICS is permitted a significant role in the implementation of these programmes. To state it negatively, with *no* common programmes, one can at least be sure that there is no ICS operator role in their implementation (see p. 20). But with the programme budget flowing through the ICS, the ICS has solid arguments for subsequent control with its national implementation (the 'controller role', see p. 20 above) or, in a few cases, for carrying out the implementation itself (the operator role).

That implementation role entails actual influence is well known from national administrations: the filling out of vague frameworks of decisions, the twisting of decisions in a direction unintended at the top, and so on (for example, Lundqvist, 1987, chapter 7.1). One's first impulse might be to believe that at least the former of these ways to influence would be even more widespread in an international than in a national setting. The vagueness of top-level decisions is normally a bit more pronounced internationally – consider, for example, compromise formulations in communiqués from top-level IO meetings. However, it is doubtful that the ICS should be able to exploit this vagueness to its advantage, even in those relatively few cases, where it functions as operator (Ascher, 1983, pp. 437–438). One must remember that top decisions are eagerly followed up in the implementation process by *national* civil servants, and here vagueness can actually be to the disadvantage of the ICS. It is commonly assumed that an important asset of weak actors is the existence of rules and standards to refer to – the more precise the better (for example, international law for small states). This assumption is probably even more valid for the extra weak actors like ICSs.[13]

This being said, we should make an exception, though, for non-routine areas, where quick improvization may be demanded by the logic of the situation (Lundqvist, 1987, pp. 174–175) (for example, the UN peace-keeping missions, where vague compromise directives from the Security Council give very little guidance as to the actual field operations required by an urgent situation; Skogmo, 1989). In such areas, there is no doubt that an ICS can acquire considerable leeway in turbulent situations. Member countries will not have time to interfere. Another exception could be areas with a pronounced low politics character that are not perceived as sufficiently important by national civil services to 'deserve' resources to be followed closely.

The question of implementation role also feeds back on influence in *previous* phases of the decision-making process. This can best be expressed inversely (see p. 26): if the ICS has little or no control over implementation, its position is weaker *vis-à-vis* the implementing member countries in previous phases of the process. It is more vital, then, that common decisions are reasonably acceptable to all IO member countries, also those that intend to vote against or are skeptical. Everybody knows that they can otherwise neglect their implementation, implement decisions differently than intended by the IO majority, or to a minor degree. Anticipating this pattern of behaviour, the ICS will be more cautious and, consequently, less influential in its behaviour.

The ICS implementation role, hence, has a direct bearing on ICS influence (see Figure 6). It has also an indirect bearing through the factor of growth: the stronger the role in implementation, the easier it will be to argue *vis-à-vis* the authority for increases in resources and personnel, which in turn is likely to improve influence (see further below). There is also a second indirect channel to consider: involvement in the implementation process renders, over time, the ICS with considerable expertise (including experience, that is, knowledge of precedence cases). The more *expertise* an ICS possesses relative to the IO member-countries (their IO delegations) or other clients, the more influence it will get (Scheinman, 1971, pp. 202–203; McLaren, 1980a, pp. 135–136; Ascher, 1983, p. 439; Jönsson, 1986, p. 44). Its arsenal of arguments will be improved: it will increasingly be able to refer to technical and 'impartial' arguments for its views that delegations will not always be able to see through or challenge. It should be emphasized here that it is not the technicality *eo ipso* of an area that is crucial; it is the *balance* of expertise between the ICS and member countries' bureaucracies (the expertise advantage to one or the other side).

The existence of rules/standards for the implementation process will affect the balance of expertise. Analogous to the argument above concerning vagueness versus precision is the view here that the more rules/standards for the implementation process, the more complex the pattern they constitute, and the more precise they are, the more favourable will be the arsenal of arguments available to the ICS relative to member countries.[14] This applies both to the ICS in the operator role and the controller role. A controller with only vague standards to refer to will, evidently, be in a weak position.

Also, when it comes to mediation, it is obvious that the existence of rules/ standards will be a valuable asset for the ICS when trying to heighten the lowest common denominator (active, in contrast to passive mediation). As was stressed already in the presentation of these types of mediation in Part I, a certain amount of authority (for example, expertise) on behalf of the mediator is necessary for an active mediation to succeed. A complex set of rules/ standards, perhaps even ICS designed, that can best be understood by the ICS itself can confer the necessary authority upon the ICS, or they can possess the necessary authority *eo ipso*, so that they make the contending parties leave the lowest common denominator.

In accordance with our reasoning in the present section, it will typically be in low politics that ICSs, by virtue of common programmes and hence more significant roles during implementation, have managed to build up an expertise advantage relative to member governments. This, in turn, increases their influence.

The height of politics is also relevant to ICS influence through the 'balance of sanctions' channel (see Figure 6). In low politics, the common programmes available to the IO and its ICS gives the ICS a relatively strong position *vis-à-vis* member countries and other clients. It interacts normally with one client at a time, who, naturally, is not in a position of strength, given the logic of the situation: the programmes constitute for the ICS *positive sanctions vis-à-vis* the potential recipients of programmes, that is, the clients (be they primary or secondary). Dubious administration, or outright misuse, of an aid programme, as evaluated by the ICS civil servants, may lead to a reduction in, or a denial of, future programmes. The potential threat of this nature can be assumed to be anticipated by clients and hence exert an influence on their behaviour. The significant conflict of interest is between conceivable recipients of programmes: programmes to one client passes by another one, and vice versa.

We have tacitly assumed here that the budget originates exclusively from the authority, that is, from member governments' contributions. However, the very possession of a common budget (and programme) makes it possible for an IO/ICS to attract further donors. As was mentioned already in Part I (pp. 23–4) this would, for the ICS, entail a diversification of dependence (that is, not being wholly dependent upon the authority). The balance of sanctions would tip somewhat in favour of the ICS, improving its autonomy and influence capability. Consequently, its actual influence would probably increase.

Apart from budget sanctions, the IO/ICS may also have legal sanctions at its disposal. Low politics should make member countries more inclined than high politics to concede legal sanctions to the IO/ICS, analoguous to other concessions of control mentioned previously (binding legal rules, though, can only be found within the EC, where sanctions are decided by the European Court of Justice).[15] Legal sanctions are, evidently, more manifest and credible than the budget sanctions discussed above. It is obvious that the existence of legal sanctions do strengthen the influence of the ICS (the EC Commission). The mere anticipation that the ICS might otherwise go to the Court, may be enough for a member country to follow the preferences of the ICS (the EC Commission).

To conclude so far, low politics entails a more favourable balance of sanctions between the ICS and its environment than high politics. This is due to the availability of a common budget and, even better, a diversification as to budget donors in certain cases. Also the availability of legal sanctions should be mentioned, even if this is a rare phenomenon. An improved balance of sanctions makes, in turn, for more ICS influence.

The Needs' Location and ICS Influence

We shall now turn to the second dimension of an issue-area's basic character, namely the area needs' location. It is connected, in the model (Figure 6), to ICS influence through two channels. One of them passes through the 'balance of power (sanctions)' factor that we have just dealt with in the preceding section. It can be argued that 'between needs' entails a weaker ICS than 'within needs'. In the latter case, there are (usually) humble and grateful secondary clients, whose needs are at stake. Their opportunities to complain about bad service from the ICS will, of course, vary with their distance from their respective governments; but it should be obvious that they do not have the opportunities that the clients have in case of 'between needs'. The effort to fulfil the latter entails by far the most inter-state coordination. The clients, those being coordinated, are governments (or actors very close to government); in other words, they are simultaneously authority (primary clients), who can closely supervise the quality of ICS performance that they pay for. There is no diversification of dependence (see Part I, pp. 23–4); the authority will see to it that the influence of the ICS is used for substantial purposes, the fulfilling of 'between needs', not for the safeguarding of the ICS's own political values.

Moreover, coordination is, by definition, an activity that implies very much attention and watchfulness from those being coordinated. The ICS must interact with several actors at a time. Coordination is not, like programmes (see above), a positive sanction that one can credibly threaten to withhold. The actors subject to coordination have, generally speaking, a *common* interest in its success. In case of perceived malfunction, they can conveniently put the blame on a common scapegoat, namely the ICS and its employees. So taken together, attempts to fulfil 'between needs' lead to a weaker ICS position *vis-à-vis* its environment than 'within needs'. Its influence will be more modest.

The second channel from needs' location to ICS influence passes through the factor of ICS *growth*. It pertains both to growth in the number of employees and growth in its budget. If we translate McLaren's pattern of thought to our slightly revised conceptual apparatus here, it sounds as follows:[16] 'within needs', be it education, health, or what not, are in principle insatiable, and the possibilities of arguing for budget increases to the relevant ICS are therefore extraordinarily favourable. They are less favourable in case of 'between needs'. When coordination problems between the IO member-states have been reasonably 'solved', there are absolutely limits to growth. Of course, coordination can always be improved, and programmes can be established for this purpose, but the need is far from insatiable. Hence, we can expect a lower growth rate (or none at all) in this case than when 'within needs' are at stake.

Growth is, in turn, connected to influence. Increased budget and more employees entails rising prestige (reputation) which enhances influence. Secondly, more employees leads to more channels, through which member governments (including their bureaucracies) and (other) clients can be affected in the direction desired by the ICS.[17] Thirdly, we can follow a more indirect line of reasoning: more employees entails improved promotion opportunities for individual employees (Michelmann, 1978, p. 231), that is, more significant positive sanctions for the ICS leadership vis-à-vis individual employees.[18] This affects two of the factors discussed in Part II, namely leadership and, most important, degree of career service. The better promotion opportunities (that is, the more vertical mobility for individual civil servants), the more the ICS resembles a career service. It was argued in Part II (pp. 44–5) that this improves the ICS's self-control (internationalism) and its influence capability (both directly and indirectly through self-control). Hence, the actual ICS influence should also increase.

Taken together, issue areas constituted by 'within needs' entail more ICS growth than 'between needs', in turn making the ICSs in these areas more influential.

Conclusion

If we sum up the effects of the two issue-area dimensions on ICS relative influence, we get the following result: areas of 'within needs' entail more ICS influence than 'between needs'. This follows from the better opportunities for growth (more elastic needs), and from a stronger position vis-à-vis clients (for example, the existence of secondary clients). As to the second dimension, low politics areas strengthen ICS influence by virtue of a minor role played by uncertainty avoidance (than in high politics), a more favourable balance of sanctions for the ICS (budget sanctions, perhaps even legal sanctions), a stronger implementation role for the ICS, and an ensuing expertise advantage.

On the basis of these conclusions, it is possible to indicate our expectations regarding ICS influence for each of the four basic characters of an issue area (see Figure 7). Firstly, however, we must eliminate one basic character from the reasoning: type IV. As previously mentioned, it is doubtful, if there exist any IOs and ICSs in this type of area: countries have their own high politics programmes, and they see no need to coordinate them (see also Figure 5).

If we distinguish between three degrees of influence – high, medium and low (which are, chiefly, meaningful in relative terms) – we get the following expectations for the three remaining basic characters: in case of low politics, and 'within needs' to fulfil, we expect high influence to the ICS in the area. If

The Height of Politics Needs' Location	Low Politics	High Politics
Within Countries	*I* Causes *High* Influence for the Area's ICS	*IV* Problem Irrelevant (no ICS)
Between Countries	*II* Causes *Medium* Influence for the Area's ICS	*III* Causes *Low* Influence for the Area's ICS

Figure 7 Basic character of issue area determining the ICS influence in the area

only the former condition is fulfilled, we expect medium influence, and if none of the conditions is fulfilled, we expect low influence.

The Selection of NATO Issue Areas for Investigation

Figure 8 indicates the various committees under the North Atlantic Council (or Defence Planning Committee, DPC), and should give an impression of the variety of issue areas covered by the NATO IO.[19] The influence of the NATO ICS will be analysed in three issue areas: force planning, infrastructure, and information. The reason for selecting these three areas is simply that they represent each one of our three relevant basic characters for an issue area: information type I, infrastructure type II, and force planning type III.[20] We can, hence, 'challenge' the established general issue-area model by investigating, if the influence of the NATO ICS in the three areas is high, medium and low, respectively.

The areas' mutual diversity is, in other words, a crucial reason for selecting them. It can be added, less schematically, that we would hardly be able to avoid force planning, an area that often is regarded as NATO's 'essential', most

The Influence of the International Civil Service: Where, How and Why? 79

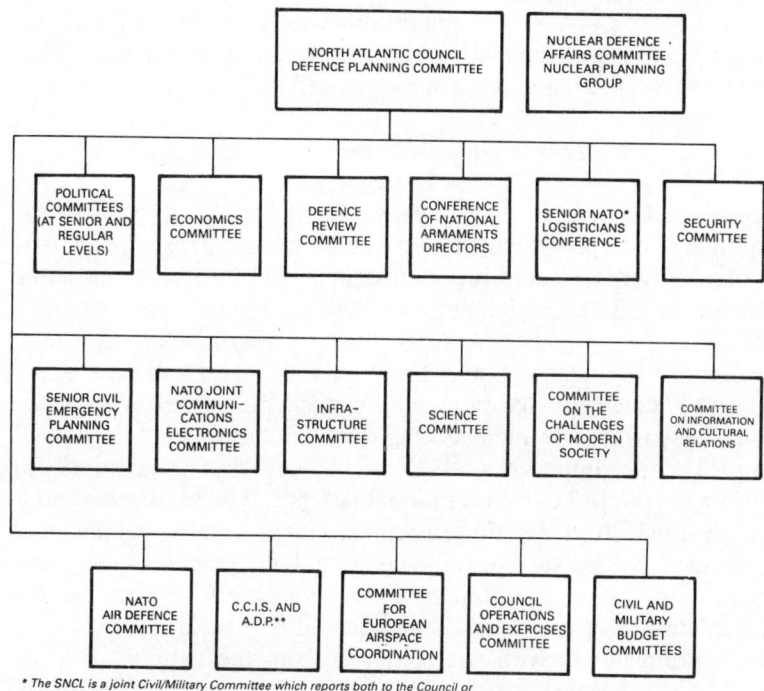

Figure 8 Committees under the North Atlantic Council

Source: NATO, *Facts and Figures*, 1984, p. 94

crucial task. It is here that the, by far, largest budgets are involved, even though they are national. Infrastructure is a remarkable field, because it actually functions supranationally; it swallows the larger part of NATO's common budget.[21] Information is interesting, among other things, because it should play both the identity role and the crucial role of conflict prevention delineated in Part I. Finally, it should be mentioned that the areas' three Directorates are the three largest NATO ICS Directorates in terms of number of employees (see Figure 11, p. 102).

Force Planning

NATO has no common defence budget. The national budgets are to some extent coordinated in a NATO setting, both as to size and content. We shall analyse NATO's decision-making in the force goals process, with special emphasis on the roles and influence of the NATO ICS (below NATO IS, that is, 'International Staff').[22] We shall see if our expectation derived from the issue-area model corresponds to reality. First follows, however, a description of the area's decision-making process in rough outline.[23]

The Decision-Making Process in General Terms

One can distinguish between three main phases in the force goals process: the ministerial guidance, the programme phase, and the review phase. In the first-mentioned phase, member-countries' ministers of defence draw up some general guidelines for defence planning. As these guidelines, however, are a compromise between 14 member countries, they are usually very vague and, therefore, provide little guidance. One of the most well known, and least vague, examples is the 1978 decision that an annual 3 per cent real increase in defence budgets should be strived for by member countries. Another example is the CDI ('Conventional Defence Improvement') effort, which gives special priority to certain deficiencies in NATO's conventional defence. The ministerial guidance is written by the IS in cooperation, of course, with national delegations and is formally decided by Ministers of Defence in the DPC for a two-year term.

In the programme phase, the military commands in NATO combine the ministerial guidance with their assessments of military needs. The process starts at the regional level, with strong inputs from the national military authorities (and a long time before the ministerial guidance has been finished). Then the assessments of the necessary force proposals are aggregated at higher levels, and priorities are decided. As regards the forces under SACEUR, the final aggregation and priorities are made at SHAPE. Even if SHAPE's assessment shall only represent the military expertise, formally, SHAPE anticipates, to a certain extent, member-countries' financial capabilities and views (Thompson and Gantz, 1987, p. 14). SHAPE's cost evaluations are made on the basis of information from member countries.

When the force proposals of the military commands are delivered to the NATO Headquarters in Brussels, the review phase starts, in which both the Military Committee (MC) and, most important, the Defence Review Committee (DRC) consider and, to some extent, modify the force proposals. The purpose is to improve the coordination of forces (for example, avoid overlappings) and to evaluate the proposals more explicitly from a political and economic perspective, than has been done previously in the process.

MC, consisting of the countries' Chiefs-of-Staff or their representatives, seldom find it necessary to exert their formal powers as the supreme military authority of the Alliance. In actual fact, a kind of rubber-stamp procedure usually takes place, where the proposals of the three MNCs (Major NATO Commands) are collected in one volume. It is difficult, of course, for the Chiefs-of-Staff or their representatives, to argue against the detailed requirements of an operational command (*ibid.*, p. 15). The functional differences compared with the operational commands may consist in MC dealing with 'political–military' issues (i 23). In controversial matters, a 'political adjustment' (i 27) may take place in MC, led by the capitals' *political* authorities. For example, in the issue of modernization of chemical weapons (1987–1988) in the US force goals, the Danish representative in the MC inserted a reservation in the report (a 'soft footnote', i 23), as an early indication of the Danish political view of the issue.[24]

The political/economic review is made by the DRC/IS. Firstly, the so-called 'trilaterals' are held, that is, meetings in member-countries' capitals between (1) defence experts from the country in question, (2) NATO's military experts (typically SHAPE officers), and (3) representatives of the IS (Force Planning Directorate). NATO's principle is that the total package of force goals must constitute a 'reasonable and realistic challenge' for member-countries' defence planning (NATO, *Facts and Figures*, 1984, p. 148); in other words, they should not be financially unrealistic, but they should imply a challenge to the country, encouraging it to an effort beyond that already planned in the country. A major set of disagreements between the three parties mentioned will then centre around, what is a 'reasonable and realistic' total package. As described by Thompson and Gantz (1987, p. 15):

> ...the nation wants to reduce the number of force proposals, the MNCs (Major NATO Commands) want the number held constant, and the IS tries to act as an 'honest broker' to reconcile the differences.

After the series of trilateral meetings, the IS civil servants write drafts of country chapters, containing a description of force proposals, their financial implications, and so on. The issues that have not been agreed upon at the trilateral meetings are emphasized.

At the so-called 'multilaterals', where the whole DRC committee is present, each country chapter is discussed with special emphasis, of course, on the remaining disagreements. When a country occupies the so-called 'hot seat', its team of experts travels to Brussels and is confronted with comments and criticism from the other countries (or some of them).[25] The countries are not ascribed veto power in their own matters (Stewart, 1985, p. 3); they can therefore be forced to acquiesce in force goals that they have not the slightest intention to implement (see below).

After the multilateral meetings, the IS rewrites the country chapters, upon which they are finally approved by the DPC. Through this approval, the force goal proposals are converted to 'NATO force goals', and as such they are introduced into the five-year planning cycle. Hence, apart from the ministerial guidance, one must say that DPC, that is, the countries' Ministers of Defence, appear on the stage at a very late moment of the planning process (Thompson and Gantz, 1987, p. 8). Apart from particularly controversial matters, the

DPC's function is mainly that of a rubber stamp. The issues have been worked out earlier.

In order to be able to exert a certain minimum of control with member-countries' implementation of commonly approved force goals, information about this implementation is obviously needed. Countries fill out a very detailed questionnaire (DPQ, 'Defence Planning Questionnaire') reporting the country's overall defence effort, and the degree to which force goals are being implemented.

On the basis of this information follows a process, which yearly, analogous to the planning process, implies a trilateral and a multilateral crossfire for each country.

We shall now proceed to analyze the roles and influence of the IS in the processes described above.

The Roles and Influence of the IS in the Process

If we start out with the bridge-building roles, it is obvious from what has already been said that the IS plays the most modest one, that of communication facilitator. Through its various service functions, it helps bring member-countries' representatives together, and through its collection of information (for example, the DPQ), and extensive report writings, it constitutes an essential element in furthering communication between them. This renders the IS a certain 'practical influence' (i 9).

Turning to mediation, the IS was cited above for being the 'honest broker' between the military commands on the one hand and member states on the other (also i 9). The military commands possess the military expertise (with a certain perspective, of course), member countries have the financial resources (and each of them a particular political/military perspective), and the IS is located in the middle with its 'practical influence' and its need to get country chapters on paper that are acceptable to all parties involved. But which type of mediation is this? According to Thompson and Gantz (1987, p. 24)

> When the civil authorities introduce compromises, they do so based on their assessment of what the traffic will bear, not on behalf of their own independent analysis of needs and priorities.

'What the traffic will bear' is exactly the essence of passive mediation as stipulated in Part I. It presupposes no authority of its own to the IS, but exactly the type of 'practical influence' that was mentioned above.

The mediator role between military authorities and member countries implies, among other things, that the IS must try to affect the latter ones in the direction of higher defence budgets (i 15). This entails that the IS in budget disagreements between member countries often may seem allied to those members that are most inclined towards higher defence expenditures, at the given time (see also Stafford, 1984, p. 158). Since at least 1979, the USA has consistently encouraged growth in defence expenditures according to the 3 per cent formula, so it is no wonder that some people have regarded the IS, at least in the questions discussed here, as being an 'instrument' of the USA. However, we are dealing with a community of attitudes, rather than an instrumental relationship. The relative 'under-representation' of the USA on the IS supports this interpretation. More important, the fact that an ICS supports a common IO decision and its implementation (in case the 3 per cent formula) does in no way require any special explanation: rather, it would seem odd, if it did not.[26]

The initiation of the CDI may seem a bit more tricky in this regard. The CDI that *appeared* to be an initiative from the Secretary General (and, hence, the IS) was in actual fact an American initiative (i 36). The Americans managed to get the Secretary-General to make it his own initiative in public. We can say, hence, that they exploited the general legitimacy of NATO and its Secretary-General to further an initiative of their own (see p. 18 on IOs as 'depositories of legitimacy'). But there is hardly any instrumentalism involved here. In actual fact, the Secretary-General would only initiate CDI if British and German support were secured in advance. As this succeeded, he agreed to go forward (i 36). Again, it seems that we have a community of attitudes. The Secretary-General, with his conditional support for the initiation idea, appears as much more than a 'tool' of the US.

As regards member disagreements different from the one on the overall height of budgets, it is difficult to imagine a too obvious community of attitudes between the IS and a certain member country (or group of countries). It can be burden sharing in a more narrow sense than the height of budgets, or burden sharing at lower levels. Each country will claim that the others do more, not only for the overall betterment of the Alliance's defence capabilities, but certainly also to shift burdens. More German ships in the Baltic will entail fewer Danish ones, *ceteris paribus*, and vice versa. In such a question, the IS can typically go in as a passive mediator (i 35), suggesting, roughly, a 'middle solution'. With its 'limited capacity for independent analysis' (i 35), it cannot come up with innovative compromise formulations, but it can mediate in the more modest way that was indicated (i 15). A mediating role is often performed by a member country, we should add (the British not uncommonly (i 15)); see pp. 57-8.

We should now turn to the roles directly instrumental *vis-à-vis* the NATO substantial values. Firstly the role as initiator. From interviews, it appears obvious that this role is *not* being played by the IS in this particular process: 'it has no weight, it cannot *create* policy' (i 15), 'it can hardly be initiator' (i 30). One might mention the CDI here as a counter-example; firstly, however, this kind of initiation is likely to be strictly limited to the Office of the Secretary-General and, secondly, as we remember, the initiative was strongly induced by one particular member country.

As stipulated in Part I (p. 20), an ICS may also play an initiating role at a more modest level than considered above. The writings of reports, both prior to and after meetings, is an initiating type of activity, and we remember from the process description that it takes place both in relation to the trilaterals and the multilaterals (notably the country chapters). There is no doubt that this activity implies the exertion of influence. This influence can be ascribed to the general and familiar psychological attachment of the participants in a meeting to an already existing draft. As expressed by Stafford (1984, p. 166; also i 9):

> one who prepares the first draft has considerable influence over the decisions eventually reached.

but also to the fact that meeting reports can confer upon formulations

> ...a final touch, a touch that will typically push in the direction of higher defence budgets. (i 15).

As summed up by one interviewee:

> The IS has a very limited capacity for independent analysis... but it does have the power of the drafted word for the country chapter as a whole and of the proposed word for disputed force proposals. (i 35)

Proceeding with the substantial roles, we should mention the role as coordinator, providing

> ...the cement in taking the contributions and getting the most out of them. (i 30).

This coordinator role continues the military authorities' efforts towards standardization, the avoidance of duplications, and so on (and should not be mistaken for the political coordination, of course). As examples could be mentioned (i 35) that the IS suggests changes in procedures (DPQ), methods of accounting expenditures, and in the definitions of terms, all of which can have policy implications. The coordinator role is relevant in all phases of the process.

As to the final phase, that of implementation, we can say that the IS activity described above can be subsumed under the observer role, that is, the most modest of the implementation roles stipulated in Part I. But the DPQ entails, though, a quite systematic type of observation.[27] Even though very much a bookkeeping exercise, one can hardly deny that the process (Thompson and Gantz, 1987, p. 18)

> ...exposes a nation's non-compliance, which could cause a nation to review its decisions, and has in the past.

On the basis of interviews and existing literature on the subject (that in no way contradict each other, but rather converge), we can establish the following list of IS roles in NATO's force goals process:

- Communication facilitator
- Passive mediator:
  (1) between NATO's military authorities and (the majority of) member countries regarding the height of budgets, entailing a certain community of attitudes with the most pro-defence member-countries;
  (2) between member-countries in other types of disagreements
- Coordinator
- Observer in the implementation process
- Initiator: not in the sense of initiating proposals, but only in the modest sense of drafting written materials

How much influence, then, is exerted by the IS? We have two sources of knowledge in this question: interview statements directly pertaining to the IS influence, and secondly the type of roles played by the IS. As to the latter, it should appear from the list above that the IS plays roles in the modest end of the spectrum, that is, those that do not imply the exertion of much influence. For instance, it is a passive mediator, and not active; it plays the least influential of the three stipulated roles for the implementation process, and it is *not* an initiator of proposals. The impression we get from this of a rather weak IS in terms of influence is corroborated by interview statements and the existing literature. The IS lacks 'an authority of its own' (i 30), 'it cannot *create* policy' (i 15). It is said, though, by one interviewee, pertaining to the force goals process as a whole:

> nations must sit down and explain... the process itself is important... we can exert pressure on them [nations]. (i 30)

Even though this statement is slightly more optimistic than the rest (the interviewee being employed by the IS), it does in no way contradict the assessment by Stafford (1984, p. 160):

> All that NATO can do is cajole and prod, and make Allied governments think twice before taking action that would weaken Alliance defences (see also Stewart (1985, p. 4) in this respect).

All our sources as to IS influence seem to converge, hence, on the view that the IS influence in the force goals process is modest, though in no way negligible. A judgement in *relative* terms, however, cannot be made before we have analysed our two other areas of concern.

Explaining the IS Influence in Force Planning

We shall now seek to *explain* the modest influence that the IS is able to exert in the force goals process. According to the general issue-area model in Figure 6, we should concentrate on the basic character of force planning as an issue area, at least initially.

As the international system is here construed – anarchic and with nation states being the primary actors, possessing a monopoly on military forces – the planning regarding the size and nature of such forces will be high politics. This will not just be so occasionally, but as long as the international system retains its anarchic constitution. In fact, force planning will probably be the 'highest' politics one can think of. Even among 'friends', a certain suspicion (uncertainty avoidance!) has been the order of the day in this area.[28] Also in established alliances, force planning has been a national concern, by and large. In no alliances (familiar to this author, at least) can be found common defence programmes and common budgets that should finance federal military forces, thereby making national forces redundant.

Turning to the needs' location, force planning in an alliance is obviously a 'between need'. In a war, the military forces should be able to move unhindered by state borders, in the light of a certain, perceived military logic and the development of war events. The relevant IO (the alliance) must therefore coordinate member-countries' force goals and the locations/movements of reinforcement forces, and work for a specialization between countries as regards certain tasks, and so on. These are, in fact, the main tasks that NATO seeks to fulfil within force-planning. It is, in other words, obviously of an inter-state nature, seeking to fulfil 'between needs'. The physical objects being moved around (McLaren's definition) are the countries' military forces.

On the basis of this dual classification of NATO force planning, its basic character as an issue area is type III (see Figure 5). The ICS in such an area will, according to the model, get a relatively low influence *vis-à-vis* its environment. From a preliminary judgement, this accords fairly well with our observation in the previous section of a modest IS influence in the force goals process.

We shall now go through those intermediate factors in the model that seem to have been decisive, in this particular case, for the relatively low influence we have found. As already mentioned there exist, by and large, only national military forces in NATO. Member nations implement their own defence policies, being more or less coordinated with other NATO member countries (and NATO institutions). The IS are only observers during *implementation*, albeit systematic and careful observers (see the previous section). In combination with the lack of sanctions in case of non-adherence to common decisions (see below), this means that the IS will be in a weak position *vis-à-vis* member states. Even though states are not ascribed veto power in their own matters in the DRC, everybody anticipates that a government can just omit to implement the commonly decided force goals, if it should so wish, for one or the other reason.

There are good grounds for believing that this anticipation affects the IS's role and influence in all the previous phases of the planning process: it serves no purpose to try to exert strong pressure on a government to accept a solution that is seen by NATO as militarily desirable, knowing that the government (or, at any rate, the parliamentary majority in the country) can ignore it later on. One must be content with posing challenges that are 'reasonable and realistic' (NATO's own formulation), given the prevailing national parliamentary attitudes, and previous experiences with the country in question.

Implementation of common decisions being left with member countries, one could, theoretically, imagine that NATO had legal *sanctions* at its disposal to safeguard a 'correct' implementation. With no supranational basis, however, there is no NATO equivalent to the EC Court of Justice,[29] not to speak of the politically unrealistic nature of such an arrangement, given the high politics nature of the area. There are no budget sanctions either, given the lack of common programmes. For instance, if Canada decides not to reinforce Norway (the Cast-brigade), the Canadian representatives will have to go through a slightly 'uncomfortable process' (i 27) of strong persuasion in the DRC and at other levels (including the DPC). But NATO has no positive sanctions that one could threaten to withdraw. Member countries, evidently, have their mutual give-and-take with relevance to the area: it has, for instance, been alleged in the Danish defence debate (1987–1988) that if Denmark did not take a larger share of the common defence burden (manifested specifically in its national defence budget, or in willingness to receive Allied ships in Danish harbours with nuclear weapons), then there would be a risk that the British reinforcement forces (UKMF) assigned for Denmark in a crisis situation would be given other tasks. The credibility of this type of sanctions notwithstanding, it should be emphasized that they are not NATO sanctions proper, but part of the general bilateral relations between member countries.[30]

Given the lack of sanctions, persuasion and argument are the only 'weapons' available to the IS (and the MNCs). But they are most effective, evidently, if supported by an *expertise advantage* to the IS *vis-à-vis* member countries. In this is included the existence of standards that member countries can be referred to. The ministerial guidance is, however, as previously mentioned, usually rather vague, and in any case too vague to be an effective instrument for the IS (Thompson and Gantz, 1987, p. 24).

The idea that one should be able to figure out an objective standard for how the military burden sharing *should* be (Birrenbach, 1962, p. 257) was abandoned a long time ago (Beer, 1969, p. 130; Olson Jr and Zeckhauser, 1970) – in fact by Lord Ismay[31] (1954, p. 94). The generally technical and incalculable nature of the subject (for example, force goals) and the inclusion of the countries' economic capabilities as a crucial factor ('no country should be called on to shoulder a defence burden beyond its means', according to NATO, *Facts and Figures*, 1984, p. 147) makes it impossible to believe that member countries should be able to agree on solutions, whose basis would be reasonably unchallenged. Even if they could, the problem for the IS would still remain that countries evidently know best about their own affairs. This gives them an expertise advantage that neither the DPQ nor OECD statistics (being used for an assessment of economic capabilities) are able to catch up with.

Arguments pertaining to national history or domestic politics are also part of member-countries' arsenal. For instance, Denmark may refer to its anti-militarist tradition of neutrality, or Canada may refer to the absence of threats to its territorial integrity in historical time and how this has affected the climate of opinion. Such arguments will, as a rule, not be accepted, and the need to 'lead' the opinion will probably be referred to (i 27, i 30). But they should illustrate the range of potential arguments in discussions on burden-sharing and related matters. The IS expertise disadvantage is, in other words, not due to lack of competence on the part of its civil servants or lack of personnel; it is built into the nature of the issue area. There will be a rich arsenal of conceivable arguments against NATO's suggested force goals in the planning process, and subsequently a corresponding arsenal of explanations, as to why the commonly decided force goals were not implemented nationally.

Thompson and Gantz (1987, p. 23) emphasize NATO's general weakness as to expertise in the area, particularly referring to the IS:

> One problem stems from NATO's weak analytic and costing capabilities which force the MNCs, MC, and DRC to depend on the nations for the input. It is thus difficult for NATO to challenge the nations at any of the formal or informal meetings. This deficiency is particularly acute at NATO Headquarters (that is, the IS and IMS, not so much the MNCs)

In interviews on the subject (two in IS, one in IMS, and one in a delegation), the evaluation is generally somewhat less gloomy. The difficulties of catching up with countries' 'natural' expertise advantage is admitted (IS); due to alleged shortage of personnel in the IS ('Directorate of Force Planning and Analysis'), 'it is often difficult to control the details and find out if they cheat' (i 9). In IMS it is said that a political 'adjustment' (i 27) of statistics may occur, but that the IS civil servants are 'well-qualified listeners', who are 'good at seeing through, if excuses hold water'.[32] It is not very surprising, of course, that IS/IMS personnel have somewhat less pessimistic views of their possibilities of solving their tasks than various outside observers. It is noteworthy, however, that even in these interviews, there are no assertions of an expertise advantage to the IS. The collection and systematization of information from countries and from OECD is an attempt to *catch up* with countries' advantage.

We have now identified a range of factors, that is, lack of significant implementation role, lack of sanctions, and expertise disadvantage that can account for the relatively low IS influence in force planning – factors that can all, ultimately, be traced to the basic character of force planning. The 'practical influence' that we observed in the previous section was ascribed, by and large, to the significant IS role in the writing of reports (the country chapters, notably). This factor is not included in our general model, as it is not supposed to vary significantly with issue areas. It is believed to confer a certain influence to all IS directorates, but it cannot be denied, of course, that it weighs relatively heavier in a directorate like the one at stake here that is generally weak on other sources of influence.

Infrastructure

By 'infrastructure', NATO understands (Van Lynden, 1974, p. 26)[33]

> ...fixed installations (with certain exceptions) in support of the operation of NATO military forces in accordance with their wartime deployment and tasks which result from the NATO approved strategic concept.

This means typically airports, military headquarters, pipelines, radar stations, harbour facilities for the reception of reinforcement forces, and so on. Countries have infrastructure of their own for their forces outside a NATO context; our interest here pertains to the commonly financed infrastructure, which can be used by the forces of other member countries and are regarded as serving the common military interests of the Alliance.[34] The justification of the principle of common financing, from a burden-sharing point of view, can be illustrated by a comparison of, on the one hand, countries like Norway and Turkey and, on the other, the USA and Canada (van Lynden, 1974, pp. 26–27). The two former countries are militarily exposed flank countries, which consequently are ascribed a significant need of infrastructure. But they have little possibility of financing it themselves, either due to low population density (Norway) or due to low GNP per inhabitant (Turkey). The two latter countries have, for purely military-strategic reasons, very little need of NATO-funded infrastructure in their countries. Their military forces operate, to a large extent in, for example, Europe and do here make use of other countries' infrastructure. Their financing abilities, that is, their GNP per inhabitant, are among the very best in the Alliance. This comparison should illustrate the absurdity implied, from a burden-sharing perspective, if each country should finance all infrastructure in its territory, that is, also the one that is seen as serving common military interests.

A positive effect from the common financing, frequently emphasized by NATO, is its political–symbolic value (for example, van Lynden, 1974, p. 26) – its identity role, the 'spirit of mutual understanding and joint purpose' – that it sustains (formulation by Lord Ismay, 1954, p. 124).[35] A tangible side-effect, for the installations' host countries, is the civilian one: employment (if the installations are built by the local labour force), improvements to the local transport system and various facilities (for example, telecommunications), and so on. There are also certain disadvantages, but judging from country representatives' efforts to acquire projects to their countries, they perceive significant net advantages from hosting projects/installations.

Compared with defence planning, much fewer economic resources are involved in infrastructure: its budget constitutes between 0.5 and 1 per cent of member-countries' total defence expenditures (van Lynden, 1974, p. 26; Thompson, 1984, p. 22); on the other hand, it swallows the major part of NATO's common budget: more than twice (in 1984) the civilian and military budgets together (Thompson, 1984, p. 20).

In this chapter, we shall analyse the IS roles and influence in the infrastructure decision-making process. Firstly, however, we must describe, in rough outline, the decision-making process more broadly.

The Decision-Making Process in General Terms

Analogous to force planning, NATO has long-term planning in the area of infrastructure, planning that is carefully coordinated with force planning and the needs for infrastructure that it has brought forward (Thompson, 1984, pp. 20, 24; *Manual*, chapter 2). The annual infrastructure programmes, so-called 'slices' in NATO terminology, are derived from this long-term planning and its 'slice groups' (at present covering six-year periods).

DPC approves, after suggestion from MNC[36] and recommendation from IC (the 'Infrastructure Committee') an economic ceiling for each slice group. In addition, IC recommends to the DPC a cost-sharing formula between member countries, prescribing how much each country shall contribute to the budget (expressed as a percentage) (Manual, chapter 4). These two decisions are, roughly, the only ones that, in *actual* fact, are politicized at the level of defence ministers.

Typically, five to six years elapse between a project being recommended and its completion. The Ministry of Defence in the potential host country for a project receives project proposals from the country's military authorities and from potential user countries' Ministries of Defence (that is, countries whose military forces shall make use of the project). In addition, there is lobbying from secondary clients such as industries with a vested interest in certain projects, and local politicians, who see a chance of getting a project, with its civilian fringe benefits, to their area. The project proposals, constituting a slice, are then sent from the host-country's Ministry of Defence to the relevant regional NATO command (MSC, see Figure 9), and, in turn, from here to MNC (for example, SHAPE). In the commands are made project priorities and, notably in SHAPE, a reduction, postponement, or rejection of certain projects. This happens with due regard to the ceiling approved by the DPC and, of course, the existing guidelines for projects' eligibility. SACEUR, being the leader of SHAPE, plays normally a crucial role in this process (Hellebust, 1974, pp. 69, 180; i 22).

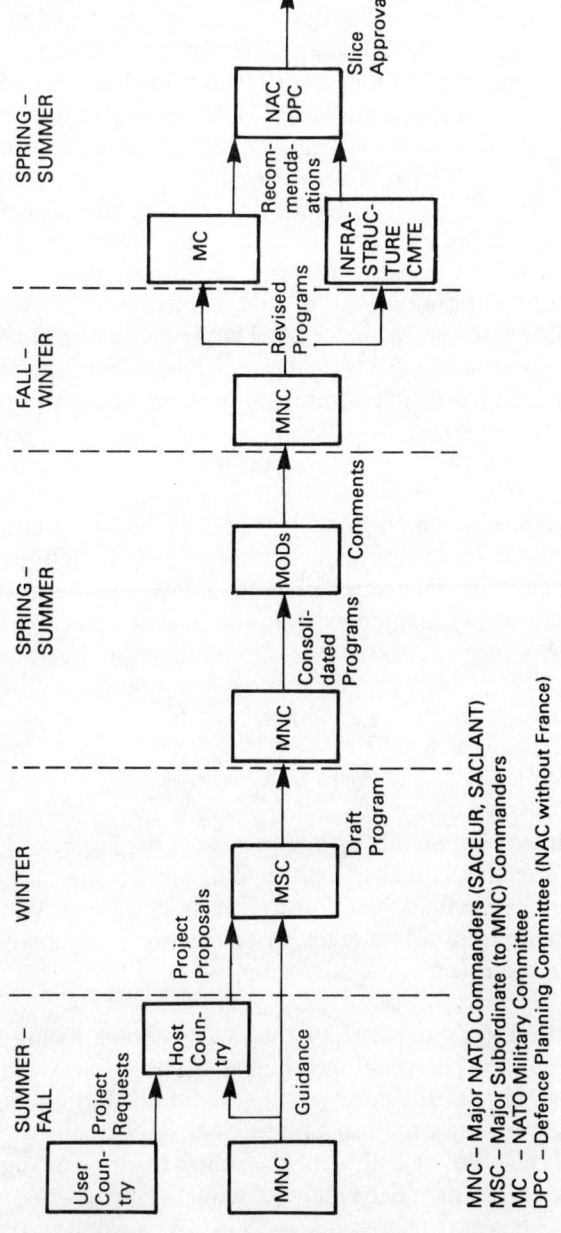

MNC – Major NATO Commanders (SACEUR, SACLANT)
MSC – Major Subordinate (to MNC) Commanders
MC – NATO Military Committee
DPC – Defence Planning Committee (NAC without France)

Figure 9 NATO infrastructure programming cycle

Source: Manual AC/4-M/206, Part I, Appendix B to Chapter 3

After consultations about the revised slice programme with Ministries of Defence, it is sent to NATO Headquarters in Brussels. It is screened here, militarily, in MC, even though one has seldom revised the project priorities made by SHAPE (i 16, i 18, i 38). The economic and technical screening is made by the IC, supported by the IS's Infrastructure Directorate. The engineers employed here write an evaluation for each project. Then a common recommendation is made for the IC and MC that is presented to the DPC and approved here as a pure formality (Hellebust, 1974, pp. 74–75). The same applies to the subsequent approval in the countries' parliaments. At this stage, almost two years have elapsed from the first presentations of the recommended projects.

Then follows the phase of detailed planning and implementation. The IS draws up, on the basis of host countries' proposals, a detailed planning and cost estimate for each project. This is sent to the 'Infrastructure Payments and Progress Committee'[37] with attached recommendations. These being approved here, appropriations can be released to the responsibility of national authorities (Ministries of Defence).[38] These must, as a rule, invite tenders for the projects (ICB, that is, 'International Competitive Bidding', see *Manual* chapter 7, p. 16). Companies from any member country participating in the funding can give tender for a project. Under certain, not very clearly stipulated circumstances, it is possible for a host country to get exemption from ICB. In any case, however, there is a strong tendency for projects to be allocated to companies in the host country, except though for highly technological projects, often going to US companies (Beer, 1969, p. 183; Hellebust, 1974, p. 182).

In the construction phase and after the termination of the work, inspections are made by, notably, engineers from the IS and SHAPE officers (*Manual*, chapter 8). IS writes a report that is submitted to the 'Payments and Progress Committee' (IPPC). Infrastructure accounts are checked by a NATO International Board of Auditors[39] and national auditors.

The Roles and Influence of the IS in the Process

As should already be roughly apparent, most of the IS's roles in the infrastructure decision-making process can be found in its later stages, the detailed planning and the implementation of projects. However, we shall see firstly whether it can play a role already in connection with the ceiling and cost-sharing discussions for a new slice group.

Ceiling   One might speculate that the IS role here is analogous to the one in discussions on the size of defence budgets. The military authorities (MNC, SHAPE) tend, not surprisingly, to suggest significantly higher ceilings than member countries, or the majority, find economically realistic.[40] Regarding the slice group 1985–1991, a ceiling of six billion IAU[41] was suggested from the military side, while member-countries would only accept a ceiling of three billion IAU.[42] It is easy to imagine the IS in this question as a passive mediator between the military expertise on the one side and member countries on the other, possessing the financial resources. Judging from the experience in the force planning field, one should imagine that the IS attitude would correspond roughly with those countries in favour of the highest ceiling. Jordan (1967, pp. 285–286) points in this direction, when saying about infrastructure:

> Although in its early stages the Programme showed signs of being dominated by the military side of NATO, after the principle of civilian control was laid down, close cooperation developed between the military planners and the civilian technicians [that is, IS]. Some tension always existed, for the civilians tended to dampen the enthusiasm of the military people.

This 'dampening' means in the present interpretation that the IS civil servants 'prepare' the military people for the member-countries' attitudes to ceiling. This interpretation, however, is contradicted in one authoritative interview (i 38):

> The question of ceiling is so 'political' that the IS civil servants can have no opinion, not to speak of influence, in this regard.

It seems, then, that our speculation implying an analogy to force planning is misleading. There is no real evidence for an IS role in the question of ceiling – quite the contrary.

Cost sharing Just as with defence planning, the conclusion has been reached regarding infrastructure that an objective burden-sharing formula is impossible to establish. The difference between the two areas is, however, that the common infrastructure budget necessitates a cost-sharing formula – and, moreover, these costs must actually be covered to their full extent.

There has been agreement on some relevant *criteria* for a cost-sharing formula: the countries' contributing capacity (GNP), advantages accruing to user nations, advantages to host nations (for example, the earning of foreign currency, employment, civilian use of the projects), and so on. But how to measure these criteria exactly, not to speak of their mutual weighting, has expectedly never been agreed upon (Jordan, 1967, pp. 268–269; Hellebust, 1974, pp. 34–35, 183; and *Manual*, chapter 4, p. 3).

Recognizing the impossibility of an objective solution, it was entrusted with NATO's first Secretary-General, Lord Ismay, to suggest a cost sharing formula. Lord Ismay himself describes his method in the following way (cited from Jordan, 1967, pp. 271–272):

> They dumped the whole problem in my lap, so I called in three Assistant Secretaries-General, and each of us drew up our own list of what we thought the percentage of sharing should be, and then we averaged them out. I couldn't for the life of me possibly say on what basis I acted, except that I tried to take into account all sorts

of things like the ability to pay and whether the building would be going on in a country so that it would benefit from the construction and the money spent. Then we got into the Council meeting in April of 1953, and everybody around the table thought that it was a jolly good distribution except for his own, which they thought was too high. Anyway, we went round the table and finally got agreement of each to take what was given within 1.8 per cent of the total, and then we simply divide up that 1.8 per cent among the fourteen, and that's all there was to it. That's why all the shares are in those funny percentage amounts.

This is actually a paradigm example of 'active mediation': as the parties recognize that they cannot solve the problem themselves, they leave the initiative to the Head of the IS, whose proposal is then, notwithstanding its more or less mathematical genesis, able to create the necessary consensus, supposedly by virtue of the Secretary-General's authority and reputation in the Council.

The cost sharing that was established at the occasion described here has, by and large, been retained ever since, with the adjustments caused by countries' entry or retirement from the cooperation. Belgium attempted around 1980 to get its share revised; after years of negotiations, the second decimal in the percentage rate was revised (i 16). In other words: revisions are next to impossible to accomplish, when so many members have veto power; *status quo*, on the other hand, has everybody learned to live with, with more or less enthusiasm.[43] So NATO still lives, in rough outline, with the results of the IS's active mediation in the beginning of the 1950s.

Programming of a slice   The IS screening of a slice prior to its approval in the DPC is described in the *Manual* (chapter 3, pp. 12–13) as follows:

> ...the IS will satisfy itself that the military requirements are met with the greatest economy to NATO, especially by looking into the following questions:
>
> a) whether military requirements cannot be met by means of existing installations from the national programmes or existing facilities, national or NATO, in course of construction, and whether neither earlier slices of infrastructure nor national programmes will be sufficient to meet the purpose;
> b) whether the purposed projects represent the most rational and economic means of satisfying military requirements;
> c) whether any suggested amendments to the recommended project acceptable to MNC should be recommended for approval by national authorities
> d) whether the cost estimates submitted are as accurate as possible; whether the applicable NATO criteria are followed and whether appropriate methods are proposed in the construction of projects;
> e) where projects may be of economic and operational national interest to the host countries, whether this interest is assessed as accurately as possible from a technical and economic point of view as a basis for recommendation of an appropriate cost sharing.[44]

Making priorities between projects, and the allocation of projects to member countries, that is, the real 'hot stuff' in a slice programming, has already taken place in the MNC (SHAPE) (*Manual*, chapter 3, p. 8). The IS role consists in an economic/technical elaboration of each single project, as described in the points above.[45]

The one point with the most potential for conflict or disagreement is probably (e) concerning the economic and operational utility value of the project for the host country. Just as with burden sharing, this utility is difficult to verify and quantify. In this and related situations, one can imagine a kind of 'information battle' between countries. As expressed by Hellebust (1974, p. 124):

> Special information on advantages to a host country from a particular project, may be the subject of concealment and/or manipulation. Host countries will typically provide a rather low estimate of their own economic and industrial advantages from a project. According to interviews, there are examples of several countries, including Norway, who have manipulated informations on civilian advantages from certain projects.
>
> Other countries' delegations, however, will be watchful, and often acquire alternative informations in order to prevent host countries from winning unfair advantages.

The British, the Germans, the Dutch and, of course, the Americans are those that have the best capacity to provide alternative information and, hence, 'supervise' others' projects (i 38). In information battles as described here, it is evident that the IS's recommendation of a 'proper' cost sharing for a project will be of the greatest importance for the outcome in the IC. The recommendation will represent the role of active mediation.

In cases where other countries do not have capacity or interest to 'supervise' a project (for instance due to its low precedence effect), the IS recommendation will be decisive. We get a bilateral relation between the IS and the host country (its Ministry of Defence), in which IS exerts an expert, and later on, a controller role. The IS will often, in connection with cost sharing, accept considerable civilian utility values for projects in the poorest countries of the Alliance (i 18, though doubted somewhat in i 38).

Exemption from ICB As previously mentioned, a host country may be granted exemption from ICB (*Manual*, chapter 7, p. 29):

> The general rule is the submission of all infrastructure projects to ICB. However, the IPPC, on request of the host nation, may agree exemption from ICB on a case-by-case basis.

As appears, there is no guideline for the granting of exemption. By national competitive bidding and, even more, 'Sole Source Procurement', one gets a much simpler procedure than ICB. The real motive behind attempts to avoid ICB, though, is often to protect the host country's own industry.

If there is not agreement in the IPPC, no dispensation is granted. In other words, if a single country is against, there will be ICB. This system obviously invites 'horse trading' between countries, in which they exchange dispensations to each other's projects. One could imagine a central role to the IS here, by virtue, for example, of its firm knowledge of precedence cases. Interviews indicate, however, that this is *not* the case. According to a delegation expert in infrastructure, the IS will 'not even recommend' a certain solution (i 16, i 18).

Inspections   A part of the IS engineers' work consists in inspection travels.[47] Projects are inspected both in the construction phase and upon completion. At the latter occasion, the inspection team is headed by the IS representative and consists, moreover, of representatives from the host country, the user country and SHAPE (MNC). The representative (*Manual*, chapter 10.2) shall supervise the project's

> ...technical adequacy, quality and economy of work and the extent to which completed construction exceeds or falls short of the scope of construction agreed upon for common financing, taking account of advice from the Military Commands and user nations as to operational acceptability.

IS then writes a report that is submitted to the IPPC. When errors and deficiencies have been corrected, and potential appropriations have been given to non-authorized work ('excess work'), the installation gets NATO's formal acceptance.

As should appear from the above, the IS role here is an expert (controller) role rather than a role as bridge-builder between member countries. Certainly, the reports must be finally approved in the IPPC. But this consists of laymen without engineering expertise and appears, as described, on the stage at a late point in time. Hence, one must assume that it is the IS that, in actual fact, stands for the control and acceptance of the installations. One *could*, of course, imagine that bridge-building would take place in certain military operational questions, between the host country and the user country; but in this type of questions, MNC officers would also be available as bridge-builders. The economic and technical control must be assumed, mostly, to be a bilateral relation: the IS controls that the host country's Ministry of Defence has administered its responsibility correctly.[48]

The IS says in a paper (p. 11) to its newly employed engineers about their working duties:

> Most engineers have learned to work with well-defined standard specifications indigenous to their countries of origin. Such well-defined standards do not exist for NATO work as such. The NATO criteria and standards usually define only in very general terms the physical scope and leave it to the host nation engineers to

determine how the NATO requirement will be met, applying national standards and methods of construction.

Consequently, Staff experts must be flexible enough to accept a variety of methods and designs, so long as the minimum military requirement is met and the solution is cost effective.

The Staff expert does not have the authority to override the judgements and designs of national MODs [Ministries of Defence], and he can only persuade and convince technical staffs in cases where his preferred solutions are different from those proposed by national experts. In other words, diplomacy is required.

Even though one must assume that a certain downplaying is made in this paper, to be read by newly employed civil servants, of their influence and controller role, the formulations should clearly illustrate the delicate position they find themselves in. In contrast to most other areas, in infrastructure specific decisions about tangible matters have to be made. Disagreements can hardly be hidden behind rhetorical compromise formulations. Even though major GNP values are not at stake, national/industrial prestige is likely to be in many cases.

The engineer has at his disposal the directorate's 'authority of its own', based on a technical and financial expertise and on its general reputation with member countries (i 10). Notably in connection with projects with few standards to refer to, the engineer must draw on the IS general reputation. The risk that he shall 'overplay his hand' (i 10) is, however, significant (the paper cited is probably designed to forestall this situation); it has happened, for instance, that national civil servants or engineers have been offended over the expression 'bad engineering' and have complained through the national channels, upon which the ambassador of the country in question has protested. The IS civil servants must, of course, be incorruptible, but they should not be stiff and inflexible. More flexibility than in other directorates is required, and often it is necessary to compromise with the quality of certain installations, not least in the poorest countries of the Alliance (i 10).

An installation's residual value   If the utility to NATO of an installation after a certain period is regarded as exhausted (or other special reasons are at stake), the host country can take over the installation, sometimes on payment of a certain sum to cover its 'residual value', that is, the value that the installation is still assumed to possess for the country in question (typically its civilian utility value). The IS has a 'very important role' (i 10) in this connection: its engineers inspect the installation and make an 'objective, technical assessment' of it (i 16), in order to evaluate its residual value. There seems, though, to be a certain room for manoeuvre and political judgement in this type of questions, at least according to delegation interviews (i 16):

- We gave them [that is, the IS engineers] some nice trips out there;
- We got the installation assessed to zero-value, even though it has, subsequently, been useful for civilian purposes.

It should be said here, though, that it is not uncommon to stipulate a zero-value, also in cases where one knows that the installation, in actual fact, has a certain civilian utility (again, mostly in the poorest countries of the Alliance).

Just as with cost sharing of singular projects, the question is whether other countries than the host country have enough capacity and interest to involve themselves in residual value issues. France's secession from most of the infrastructure cooperation in the 1960s led to a tough and fatiguing tug-of-war concerning the residual value of the French installations, in which the USA was France's adversary, with the IS 'at the side-line' (i 18) (see Beer, 1969, pp. 184, 198–200). This is, though, a somewhat special case, given the large amount of infrastructure installations that had been built in France. Normally, the residual value is evaluated for one installation at a time. It is dubious here, if countries other than the one directly involved will go seriously into an 'information battle' (see p. 95, though). At any rate, just as with 'normal' inspections, we can probably ascribe the IS an expert and controller role, bilaterally in relation to the country in question.

Conclusion: the roles and influence of the IS in the process On the basis of the above analysis, we can establish the following list of IS roles in the infrastructure area:

- Active mediator:
  Between member countries at the original agreement on a cost-sharing formula (that, by and large, has been retained since then)
- Expert and controller role:
  Regarding the programming of a slice, the screening of project applications, inspections of installations, and the evaluation of installations' residual value
- Identity role:
  The symbolic value of the very existence of a common-financed programme

One could add to these roles some more modest ones that the IS plays in infrastructure, just like in defence planning: communication facilitator, coordinator, and initiator by virtue of the writing of reports. The rest, however, is different: the IS has, in a very crucial matter, played the roles as active mediator in infrastructure, and the IS has, in this area, a markedly stronger role as expert and controller.[49]

How much influence, then, is exerted through the playing of these roles? Compared with defence planning, more influential roles are at stake this time: active mediation, not only passive, and a strong controller role in several of the phases described, versus the observer role in defence planning. This conclusion is corroborated through a range of interview statements, some of which have already been cited: in contrast to force planning the IS has in infrastructure an 'authority of its own' (i 10), which, of course, must be exerted cautiously (see above). Even though infrastructure is a very limited field in budgetary terms compared with force planning, decisions are made and influence exerted on tangible issues. The agreed ceiling must actually be reached, the cost sharing must be respected, deficiencies with the installations must be corrected, and the residual value for an installation must actually be paid, and so on. Within its limited field, the IS infrastructure directorate appears according to interviews as stronger than most other IS directorates in their respective fields. Among four interviewees (two delegation civil servants, one IS infrastructure civil servant, and one IS defence planning civil servant), they all rated, without the slightest 'guidance' from my side, the infrastructure directorate as the relatively strongest *vis-à-vis* member countries. It is 'different from all the others' (i 9), 'the best of all fields' (i 14).[50]

Explaining the IS Influence in Infrastructure

We shall now seek to *explain* the relatively high influence that the IS is able to exert in infrastructure and, in particular, why it is more influential here than in force planning. We shall, hence, focus at the basic character of infrastructure, as prescribed by the issue-area model (Figure 6).

Firstly, is infrastructure high or low politics? Even though military matters are traditionally regarded as high politics (see defence planning), it seems that infrastructure, perhaps due to its marginal budgetary size, is not so perceived by national top decision-makers. It has been mentioned that the area is, by and large, delegated by ministers to civil servants; also, it is not an issue debated in parliamentary assemblies. Apart from certain specific issues that may turn up,[51] only the questions of cost sharing and ceiling are, occasionally, dealt with by ministers.[52] Indicative of a (relatively speaking) low politics status is also the fact that member countries have accepted the uncertainty implied by a common budget and common programmes. Therefore, we shall classify the area here as one of low politics.

Secondly, is NATO infrastructure a need between countries or within countries? As here conceived, it is obviously the former: the establishment of installations that are necessary, for example, for the reception of reinforcement forces from Allied countries. As we remember, the 'common use' projects are given higher priority than 'common interest' projects; in other words, the most crucial installations are those that can also be used by the forces of other countries.[53] The physical objects (McLaren's definition!) that, in virtue of the infrastructure installations, can be transported between countries, are aeroplanes, ships, fuel, communication signals, and so on.

On the basis of this dual classification of NATO infrastructure, its basic character as an issue area is type II (see Figure 5). The ICS in such an area should, according to our model, be able to exert a 'medium' level of influence, relatively speaking, *vis-à-vis* its environment. What can be said at this stage is

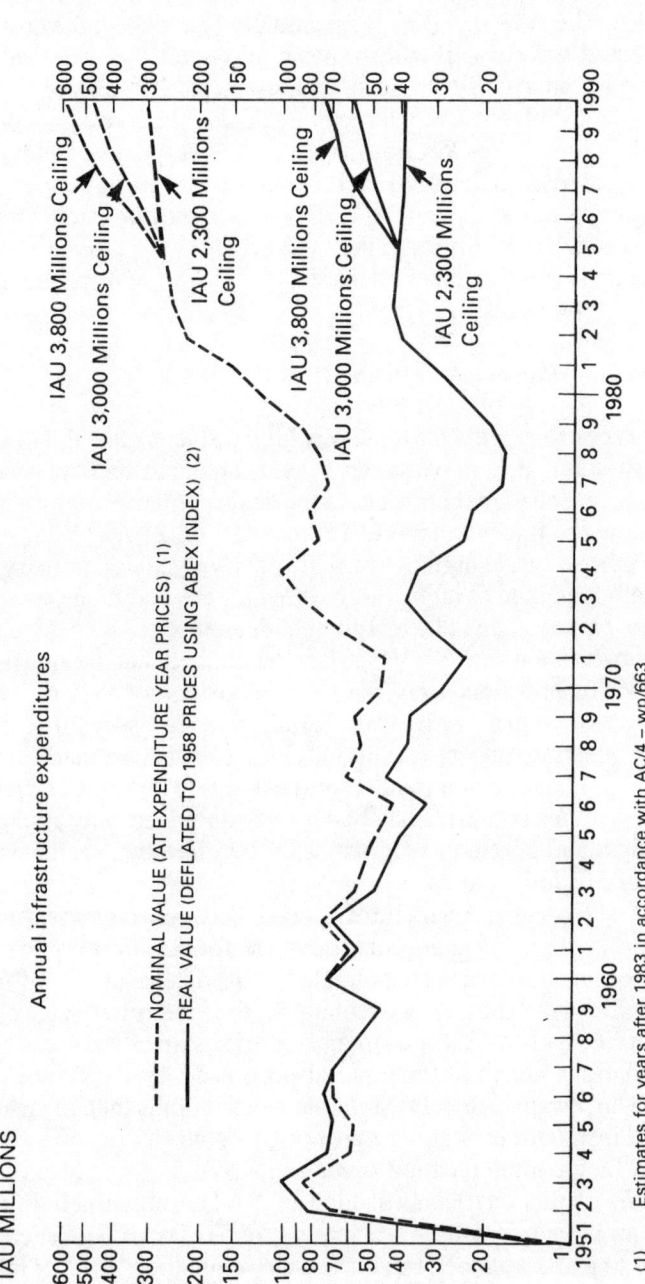

Figure 10 Nominal and real values of annual NATO infrastructure expenditures

that it seems to correspond, roughly speaking, to our observations: the IS does *not*, in infrastructure, play the most influential roles such as operator during implementation or initiator of projects; on the other hand, we have described it as significantly stronger in this area than in defence planning, where only the most modest roles are played.

We shall now indicate those intermediate factors in the model that seem to have been decisive, in this particular area, for the level of influence being exerted. The fulfilling of 'between needs' should lead us to expect a rather modest growth, if any, in budgets and number of employees in the Infrastructure Directorate. Regarding the former, the expectation seems to hold true until about 1980. As appears from the 'real value' curve in Figure 10 there has actually in this period been a slightly falling tendency in the budget. The explanation is (i 16) that a certain satiation occurred, as the first, relatively urgent installations had been established: air fields, war headquarters, fuel supply systems, harbour facilities, and so on (see also Beer, 1969, pp. 179, 203). As expressed by Jordan (1967, p. 286):

> It was at first assumed that the Infrastructure Programme would be self-liquidating, that is, once the fixed installations were built the work would be finished.

From about 1980, however, a relatively significant growth sets in, due, among other things, to the breakthrough of electronics and the increased weight to the communications field.[54] Furthermore, a gradual extension of the criteria of eligibility for projects takes place. Hence, in contrast to what Beer notes in 1969 (p. 203), a certain task expansion has now taken place. The expectations among insiders to the area are today also entirely different from the citation from Jordan above. It is stressed in interviews that the need 'will never be filled' (i 18), there is 'no upper limit' (i 22), it will 'go on ad infinitum, though not steeply' (i 26). In other words, we are now in a more 'normal' situation for budgets than during the first 30 years of the Alliance.[55] Our expectations pertaining to 'between needs' areas, hence, did only hold true for the first three decades; then, exogenous factors, primarily the technological development, confers an elasticity upon the needs at stake, making them resemble intra-state needs.

Whether budget growth in recent years has had an independent impact on IS influence is hard to say. One can assume, however, that it has implied increased prestige for the directorate and its civil servants.

Turning to the number of employees, infrastructure had in 1987 46 A-grades, whereas defence planning (= 'force planning') had 23. As appears from the figures in Figure 11, infrastructure was actually the largest among the IS directorates. It has grown from 40 A-grades in 1975 (whereas force planning has witnessed a standstill in the same period). Even though one should always be cautious in drawing inferences from figures like these, it can be said, at any rate, that the number of civil servants accords fairly well with the Infrastructure

102   *The International Civil Service*

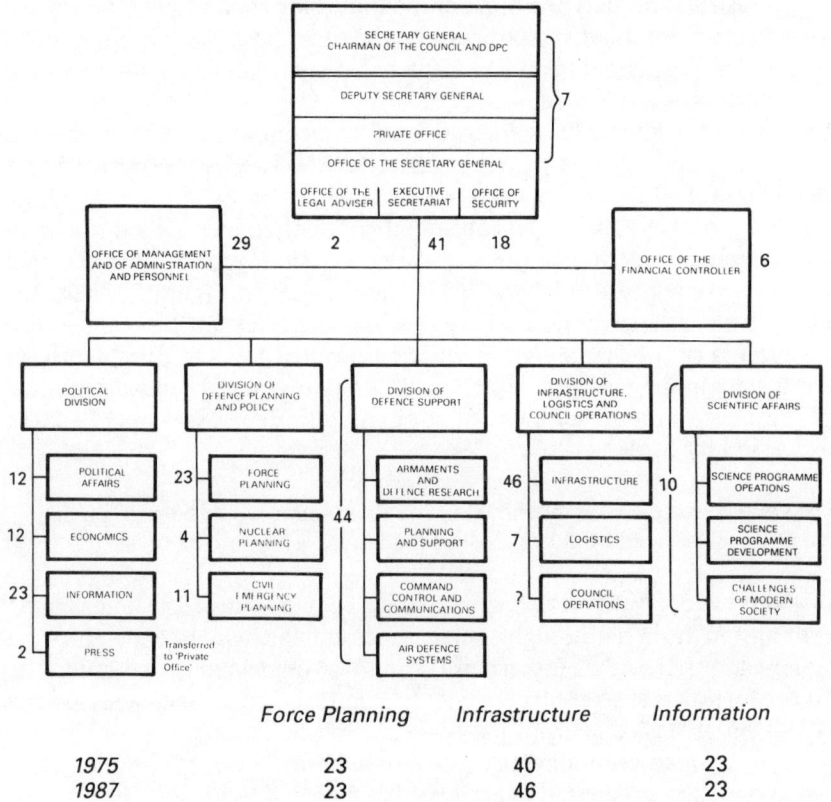

Figure 11 The number of A-grades in IS Directorates, and the long-term trend for three selected Directorates

Sources: The upper part is from NATO's *Facts and Figures*. The inserted figures have been computed on the basis of *Organizational Charts 1987*, based on Document C–M (86) 79 (NATO unclassified). The trend figures have been supplied by the NATO Information Service (1990)

Directorate's relatively significant influence (in comparison, for instance, with defence planning). It will not, however, be regarded as a factor with any crucial explanatory power of its own. As we shall see, there are other factors that can carry the burden of explanation more easily.

We have analysed, in the previous section, the influence exerted by the IS during the implementation of projects, notably through the roles of expert/controller. Lack of interest or capacity on behalf of member countries was seen, in some questions, as strengthening the IS influence. In addition to this influence, the IS role during implementation has also led to a significant *expertise advantage vis-à-vis* member states (see Figure 6), for one thing, in the simple sense that it has necessitated the employment of a large technical (engineering) and economic expertise.[56] Of the 46 A-grades employed in 1987, 36 were engineers. It was noted by an external observer that the IS engineers, as a rule, are competent people.[57]

The IS's 'technical and financial expertise' gives it the 'authority of its own' that we have previously registered. This authority also springs from the fact that a complex, though relatively precise, set of standards (criteria, guidelines) are available as support: 'We have the standards', 'our field is more tangible than the others' (i 10). As described in the *Manual* (chapter 6, p. 1):

> Criteria for NATO common infrastructure projects are developed to define the scope of works that may be authorised to meet justified NATO minimum military requirements... and to outline technical guidance for those authorised works.... Criteria provide engineering guidance, rules and technical characteristics which constitute standards to be applied during the planning and implementation of infrastructure projects.

Moreover, the IS has had an important role in the drawing up (and the current revision) of these criteria (as regards the military criteria, though, the MNCs have, not surprisingly, been more important). In decisions on deviations from existing criteria, the IS has also a crucial role (*Manual*, chapter 6, p. 5).

In certain cases, one must do without rules (*ibid.*, p. 2):

> Some categories of infrastructure, because of the varied nature of the works involved, do not lend themselves to the development of a uniform set of criteria. Projects in these categories are judged and evaluated on a case-by-case basis.

Then, the IS must instead rely on its general 'reputation with nations' (i 10). The *Manual* describes these situations as follows (ibid., chapter 8, p. 9):

> ...When there are no precise standards, the host country is responsible for ensuring that good engineering is utilised in carrying out a NATO infrastructure project.

It is evident that the IS position is weaker here: 'good engineering' is an amorphous concept. The special diplomatic skill that was stressed in the paper to newly employed engineers, is probably the most required in such cases.

Another underpinning for the expertise advantage is that IS infrastructure civil servants remain for relatively lengthy periods in their jobs, both compared with their colleagues in other IS directorates and MNC officers. In the paper referred (p. 96), it is said that

> ...since NATO military representatives normally rotate every two (or three) years, the International Staff members provide the only continuity in Infrastructure matters, and consequently must have the patience to explain to each new military 'generation' the way the game is played under NATO rules.

The advantage as to, notably, experience that can be assumed to spring from this continuity is, of course, important. But it exists only *vis-à-vis* MNCs (SHAPE), not in relation to member countries and their delegations. There is a tradition here, just like in the IS, that civil servants dealing with infrastructure remain in their posts for longer time periods than their colleagues in other fields (Hellebust, 1974, p. 83).

It should be stressed, finally, that the experience and expertise that the IS gets from its implementation roles is also instrumental in other phases of the process: the programming of slices, appropriations, and evaluations of installations' residual value. A knowledge of the typical problems in connection with inspections is, of course, useful at the programming of new projects.

In comparison, while the IS in defence planning seeks to catch up with countries' expertise advantage in their own affairs, it has in infrastructure an expertise advantage *vis-à-vis* the same countries. In spite of flexible or lacking rules in some cases, the general picture should be obvious: by virtue of its technical and financial expertise, and by virtue of the set of criteria and guidelines that it has itself often drawn up, the IS possesses a firm argument base *vis-à-vis* member countries. This base must be one of the main explanations for its influence in the area.

Turning to the *balance of power* (*sanctions*) between the IS and its environment, it is obvious that NATO possesses significant positive sanctions. NATO has projects, with attached civilian fringe benefits, to be allocated. In theory, hence, there exists the threat of withholding the positive sanctions in the future, in case of unsatisfactory national administrations of projects (as evaluated by NATO). This is, however, a threat that resides with the MNCs, rather than with the IS (the MNCs making priorities and country allocations, as we saw). There appear to be no cases where this latent threat has materialized.[58] And its credibility is also weakened by the fact that there are military considerations of necessity behind project priorities and their allocations in certain territories.

So when it is said in the IS that 'we have the stick', 'we can punish them [that is, member countries]', 'we have the hand on the purse' (i 10), more modest sanctions are referred to. One can omit the recommendation of certain projects 'in their present form' or, as hinted in the third formulation, one can recommend that appropriation is not granted until certain specific technical or financial problems have been solved to IS's satisfaction. With the same purpose, one can withhold the acceptance of an installation or suggest a higher degree of country financing in future projects based on cost sharing. These more modest sanctions do frequently materialize and they are also, evidently, anticipated by countries in their general dealings with the IS.

Remaining with the balance of power (sanctions), the client/authority constellation is quite unfavourable in infrastructure, as it is for NATO in general (see Part I). The clients are simultaneously authority, namely, member governments. Specifically, clients are the Ministries of Defence that are responsible for the building of installations, and the military forces (from one or more nations) that shall actually make use of the installations. These clients are close to, or even part of government; hence, they are in optimal positions both to supervise the quality of IS (NATO) 'services' and to complain, if they should be dissatisfied. This, of course, weakens IS autonomy and its possibilities of furthering its own political values.

There are secondary clients, though: firms that strive for project contracts, and local politicians, who perceive the civilian fringe benefits from a project. These two groups, however, are clients *vis-à-vis* the Ministries of Defence, primarily, being responsible for the building of installations. Hence, they do not really change the unfavourable client/authority constellation, seen from the viewpoint of the NATO IS.

To sum up it seems that the most crucial factor that can account for the IS influence in infrastructure is the IS expertise advantage in this area *vis-à-vis* member countries that has been accumulated by virtue of the IS controller role during implementation. It is more difficult to verify an independent impact from the factor of technological breakthrough (and, hence, the growth factor), and we have seen that the balance of power (sanctions) *vis-à-vis* the environment is not particularly favourable. We did mention certain sanctions, though, at the disposal of the IS, pertaining to the elaboration of projects/installations.

Information

We have observed the role as IO identity supporter being played as a byproduct to the safeguarding of other values than IO identity. For instance, the successful carrying out of a commonly funded programme like infrastructure symbolizes a certain Alliance unity or identity. The very existence of an ICS symbolizes IO identity. However, there are also structures in the Alliance whose primary purpose (substantial value) is the furthering of NATO identity. This applies, firstly, to the IS Directorate of Information, also labelled 'NATO Information Service' (NATIS). While the Press Service, belonging directly to the Secretary General's Office, deals with current NATO news and announcements, NATIS (NATO, Facts and Figures, 1984, p. 132)

> ...is concerned with providing facts through all available media about the longer-term aspects, such as why and how NATO was created, how it functions, and the general lines of agreed NATO policy.

Only a certain share of the NATIS budget is spent on its own activities; a considerable part is allocated to national information organizations, be they public or private identification actors. In addition to these two types of NATO information (identity support), we shall also analyse, below, that carried out by the NATO Secretary-General, for example, in connection with visits to member-countries. These are the three main types of NATO identity support that one can distinguish. The challenges that they have had in common during the 1980s have been, for example, the peace movements in the beginning of the decade (representing a threat scenario different from that of NATO), and the so-called 'Gorbachev effect' in the second half of the decade (that is, the popularity of the Soviet leader in Western opinion, challenging NATO's threat scenario). The Gorbachev effect has exacerbated the so-called 'equidistance syndrome' (Hofman, 1987, the NATIS Director), that is, the view among segments of the European opinion that an equal distance should be laid to the two Superpowers. Such neutralist tendencies evidently challenge the Atlantic ties that are an essential part of NATO's identity. Finally, and probably most important, should be mentioned the revolutions in East European societies taking place presently (1989–1990). With the profound implications of these for NATO, they will require major revisions of the 'message' of NATO information activities.

One of the main reasons for the importance of the role as identity supporter is the fact that it closely resembles the role as conflict preventor, as described on pp. 19–20. Also it is instrumental in relation to the bridge-building roles: the more feeling of IO identity prevailing, the easier it will be to accomplish bridge-building between the IO member countries. Given the maximum amount of bridge-building need that we have registered in the case of NATO, one can assume that the identity role is seen as crucial by NATO institutions.

We shall now, in rough outline, describe the processes through which NATO identity is sought sustained by NATO international civil servants (including the Secretary-General). Subsequently, we shall analyse how much influence is being exerted by the NATO ICS in these processes, and how this influence can be accounted for.

NATIS's Own Activities

NATIS's own activities comprise, for instance, the arrangement of visits to NATO HQ in Brussels for various groups, be it parliamentarians, chief editors, trade unionists, or students (in total about 20 000 persons per year (i 7)). Priority is given to (NATO, *Facts and Figures*, 1984, p. 133; also i 37)

...those in a position to pass on information to wider circles.

Both in NATIS and in national activities, younger persons, not least high school and university students, are given special preference (NATIS employing a special 'youth officer'). Among other activities, we should mention assistance to television companies making programmes on any aspect of NATO, publications such as *The NATO Review* (translated to all languages of the Alliance) and NATO's *Facts and Figures*, and also the administration of a NATO Research Fellowship Programme.

As with other areas, there is a special committee of member-country representatives surveying NATIS, the 'Information Committee'. However, it is quite 'different from the other ones' (i 24). It meets rather infrequently; as one critical member of it said (i 29):

...it meets only once a month and does nothing.

Moreover, the small delegations send typically young diplomats in the beginning of their careers (i 37), who simultaneously 'cover' several other committees, and therefore can hardly be experts in the field. Also, they have difficulties in getting instructions from their respective capitals. The result of this is that the Information Committee is rather weak. Nine out of ten initiatives come from the Committee's Chairman (that is, NATIS) (i 29); countries' suggestions usually can be found under 'Other Business' at the end of the meeting. What the Committee can do, hence, is a kind of 'micro-management' (i 37), retrospectively commenting upon details in the NATIS programmes. In some cases, these details may be very much 'micro' indeed: a map may highlight the Greek/Turkish conflict concerning the border line in the Aegean Sea (for example, Lemnos); the NATIS solution may then be to blur the map so as to conceal the conflict. Formulations in publication drafts are corrected; in case of country disagreements, the lowest common denominator is likely to be chosen, again concealing the problem at stake.[59]

Not surprisingly, NATIS tries to avoid detailed supervision, if possible. One committee member, rather critical of his own committee, labelled this an effort towards 'damage limitation' (i 29).[60] Or as expressed by Genton (1989) p. 25:

Unfortunately, this committee [the Information Committee] is often only moderately effective as it attempts to monitor the day-to-day activity of the Information Directorate [NATIS], which in turn tries to remain independent enough to be able to continue to act.

Member-countries' Information Activities

As already mentioned, a considerable part of information activity on behalf of NATO is not carried out by NATIS, but by national organizations. Some of these identification actors are supported economically through NATIS' budget (supplementing other, both public and private sources). The philosophy behind this rather decentralized information structure is that it safeguards the necessary familiarity with the specific national problems and target groups (see further below). There are differences of opinion among governments, though, on *how* much decentralization is desirable, the French stressing national responsibilities the most, and the US emphasizing common efforts the most. In NATIS, where one should *a priori* believe centralization to be preferred, the decentralized model is generally accepted (i 37).[61] Perhaps due to 'anticipated reaction' (i 36), there are no expansionist tendencies in NATIS. For instance, NATO Information Offices in member countries (analogous to the EC Information Offices), staffed by NATO international civil servants, have never been seriously considered, not even in the first years of the Alliance (Jordan, 1967, p. 185).

The doctrine of NATO information is that it should be bipartisan. As expressed by Lord Carrington (Astori, 1987, p. 23):

> ...these supporter organisations [the national information organizations] should, if at all possible, continue to work on a bipartisan basis as far as the domestic democratic political spectrum is concerned.

The reason for this doctrine (applying, more or less, to all three types of information activities delineated) is probably expressed by Clark (1986, p. 40), when saying that

> NATO will not survive electoral changes in member countries if it is closely identified with governments in office.

The problem is only, what 'bipartisan' (or 'impartial') are supposed to mean in cases with strongly diverging views on NATO policy between government and opposition. For instance, the lack of Danish domestic consensus on major elements of NATO policy 1982–1988 (roughly speaking) did create dilemmas for information activities (i 42). One could hardly expect NATO-supported publications to lay a distance to the NATO double-track decision of 1979 regarding middle-range nuclear missiles or the actual deployment of 1983, although a Danish 'average' parliamentary view would do so (not to speak of the parliamentary majority, opposing the government in these questions). In certain respects, a low-key posture was preferred in information activities (i 37, i 42), as a 'solution' to the dilemma described.

The national 'information situations' are reported in two committees: CONIO and MODIO. CONIO consists of the national Heads of information services from the Ministries of Foreign Affairs, whereas MODIO brings together the information officers from the Ministries of Defence. They meet even less frequently than the Information Committee: annually or biannually. No communiqués are decided upon and no decisions proper are expected to be made (i 24). Summaries of the meetings are written on the responsibility of the Chairman (= the NATIS Director), and are delivered for approval in the North Atlantic Council. The lack of a common communiqué implies that the interest in capitals is generally weak, and therefore national representatives often act on their own judgement.

Funds are allocated by NATIS, on the basis of detailed applications (and budgets) to the activities of national information organizations (on an *ad hoc* basis). It seems (i 37, i 40, i 42) that NATIS's 'liaison officers' (that is, liaison with one or more member countries each) have a crucial role to play in this process that involves, of course, the making of priorities between organizations within each country (the Information Committee is not involved (i 40)). To this comes, however, at a more aggregate level, that the NATO IS can select certain countries as 'high priority' for a given year. The funding for a country can, hence, shift considerably from year to year. Denmark, for example, got a 25 per cent 'raise' from 1986 to 1987. Out of a NATIS budget of 120 million Belgian Francs in 1987, Danish organizations actually got 18 million Belgian Francs which implied a top position in the Alliance (shared with Norway). Turning from absolute to relative figures, this first position is, evidently, extremely pronounced (that is, funding per inhabitant). The point to emphasize here is that we are not just dealing with marginal adjustments from one year to the next – quite the contrary.

In particular, the smaller member countries have opportunities for getting 'high priority' status; whereas money spent in a Great Power can easily be a 'drop in the ocean' (i 7), an effort in a Small Power can promise greater benefits, also in view of the formal NATO decision rules (p. 28). It also depends, of course, on the perceived 'need' in the relevant country. For instance, Holland was given 'high priority' status in connection with the 'missile battle' in the early 1980s, where (i 7)

...half of Holland was pulled through the NATO HQ.

The locus of priority decisions is difficult to assess from interviews. It is *not* any of the three committees in the area. The NATIS Director (i 24)

...keeps the decisions close to himself.

it *seems* that they are made between the NATIS Director, the Assistant Secretary-General for Political Affairs (see below), and the Secretary-General (i 24). They are not put on paper, at any rate.

Apart from the countries that, for a certain period, wish a 'low key' posture (see above), it can be no surprise that countries generally wish to get a high priority, and that they work through their delegations to attain this status.

NATIS also controls the activities it has funded, as far as this is possible (again, there is no role to the Committee in this). A statement like the one cited above by the Secretary-General on the principle of 'bipartisan' information is, of course, a way of providing guidelines for the NATO-supported information activities. Bipartisanship can relatively easily be controlled in publications, but it is probably almost impossible to evaluate the very *success* of the efforts (as with NATIS's own efforts). Opinion polls favourable to NATO or to specific NATO policies may, even if reliable, be ascribed to a host of other potential causal factors than the virtues of information activities. As in other ICSs, there is also in NATO a general tendency towards the devaluation of language, that is, the description of nearly all arrangements as 'outstanding' or 'tremendous successes'. However, as emphasized by one NATIS official, failures can sometimes be observed, and adjusted (i 37):

> ...if they do not come up with better programs and improve their activities, they will simply not receive support next time.

At any rate, the very detailed application procedure (i 40, i 42) together with the presentation of accounts, gives NATIS a solid grip on which specific *types* of activities are being supported.

The Secretary-General's Identity Role

We have seen several cases so far, where the Head of the IS, the Secretary-General (SG), has played significant roles as, for example, active mediator between member countries. As in other IOs, there is probably a good deal of analogy between the roles of 'ordinary' international civil servants, chairing various sub-committees, and the role of their Head in the Council (for example, Rovine, 1970, p. 436).[62]

When it comes to the identity role, the SG is especially qualified, by virtue of the symbolic significance of the Office and personal authority (for example, Jacobson, 1984, pp. 118–122). Through his press conferences, official visits to member countries (including their Heads of State), and speeches held in these connections, he has favourable opportunities for doing a PR effort on behalf of NATO. As with his roles at the more general level, where some SGs have tried to be initiators and active mediators (like Spaak, 1957–1961), while others have remained more cautious in their efforts (like Ismay, 1952–1957, or Brosio, 1964–1971), SGs have also varied a great deal, when it comes to PR efforts and abilities. But whereas the more general roles have probably varied more with external circumstances than with personalities (Jordan, 1979, p. 266), the PR abilities can be ascribed mostly to political career background, personality factors, and even such a seemingly trivial matter as native language (English, of course, providing the easiest way). The factor of personality (including working style) can be illustrated by Jordan's (1979, p. 176) description of the Italian SG Brosio's PR abilities:

> As might be expected, Brosio's conscientious methods applied to his conduct of press and public relations. Not a superficial person, he was concerned with substance, not image. The qualities he brought to the office of Secretary-General – moderation, loyalty, thoroughness, and tolerance – were not entirely suited to the demands of twentieth-century journalism. He was not a propagandist; he felt that the press generally was neither useful nor potentially harmful in the diplomatic process. Most newsmen were uninterested in Brosio: he lacked flair, his desire for accuracy was too deeply rooted to be compromised for a colorful phrase, and his use of language was too judicious to make good copy.

The Influence of the International Civil Service: Where, How and Why?

As to the third factor, that of political career background, NATO has almost always nominated SGs with a background in 'high politics', typically former Foreign Ministers. The SG being an 'outstanding international figure in his own right before his appointment' to the post (Hill, 1978, p. 33) evidently makes his information activities much easier, by virtue of an *a priori* 'natural' publicity (i 1, i 13, i 28).[63]

Even with optimal predispositions for PR efforts, however, there are certain crucial constraints on SG speeches. One of them was described vividly by Lord Carrington, at the opening of a speech in Copenhagen 1986:

> I have been Secretary-General long enough to know that making speeches is part of the job, and I try not to complain too much about that. But I do occasionally look back with a tinge of envy at the much greater rhetorical scope allowed to Foreign Ministers. They can roam the world in search of fresh subjects to address, while I must stick to my last: venturing not in the forbidden lands that lie out of area [the area described in the North Atlantic Treaty], and trespassing not in fields that are for other organizations to till.

Apart from this geographical/functional constraint, there seems to be, at least to a certain extent, a consideration for bipartisanship regarding the domestic political spectrum in a given member country (second, though, to the task of advocating NATO policy (i 43)). For instance, Lord Carrington planned a visit to Copenhagen in May 1988, in connection with an NPG meeting. However, parliamentary general elections were announced, unexpectedly, to be held shortly after the visit, the occasion being an issue regarding nuclear weapons on visiting ships in Danish harbours, but also the more general lack of consensus on Danish NATO policy. Both the NPG meeting and Lord Carrington's visit were cancelled. Various 'theories' exist on the reasons for this (i 40, i 43), but it seems fair to ascribe the cancellation mainly to the fact that a visit would unavoidably imply questions to the SG on the main election issue. And answers to these would hardly be able to be bipartisan in relation to attitudes in the Danish Parliament. As with other SGs, to (Jacobson, 1984, p. 120)

> ...appeal overtly and directly to the public of a member state for a policy opposed to its government [here: parliamentary majority] would be a venture almost certainly destined to fail.

So also in this branch of information work, a low key posture may sometimes be seen as the only way out.

An advantage accruing to SG 'visiting' speeches is the possibility of being sensitive to specific national problems and preconditions. When comparing some of Lord Carrington's speeches on the two sides of the Atlantic, it is obvious that they are 'adapted' to their respective audiences. In Europe, he would stress the need for an improved defence effort (Lord Carrington, 1986, Copenhagen):

> I should like to see Denmark doing a bit more

perhaps hinting the need for not estranging the USA. In the USA, he would emphasize the European contributions to defence, and to a certain extent defend typical Small Power views, like the following (Lord Carrington, 1984, p. 195, speech in New York City):

> ...we must beware of the temptation to short-cut procedures which reflect the fundamental, democratic nature of the alliance.

This possibility of adaptation to audiences is, of course, shared with the national information organizations.

A final question that we should address in this section is the relationship between the SG and NATIS – if any. During Lord Ismay's period, NATIS was raised to the level of a Division, reporting directly to the SG (Jordan, 1967, p. 176). The NATIS Director was allowed to attend Council sessions. Today, however, NATIS is a directorate under the Political Affairs Division (see Figure 11). The NATIS Director reports to the ASG for Political Affairs, who in turn reports to the SG. A range of newly published NAA reports, however, have argued that NATIS should be transferred from 'Political Affairs' to the SG 'Private Office' (Clark, 1986, p. 40; Astori, 1987, p. 26; and Genton, 1988, p. 27). For instance (i 39), the SG would have a much better knowledge of NATIS activities and problems and, hence, be in a stronger position in the Council (facing country ambassadors), when arguing for budget increases or more NATIS autonomy *vis-à-vis* member countries. As it appears, however, the SG has acquiesced in *status quo* (Astori, 1987, p. 23), perhaps partly due to strong opposition to the suggested reform from the ASG for Political Affairs (i 39).[64]

The Roles and Influence of the IS in Information

We shall now draw together our observations concerning the roles and influence of the IS, that is, NATIS and the SG, in their activities towards furthering NATO identity (being the substantial value to be safeguarded in the area). It seems that the following roles have been played:

- Initiator: NATIS's own activities (9 out of 10 proposals coming from NATIS itself).
  Proposing, or rather *deciding*, on the budget allocations to national information activities between countries and between organizations.
  The SG's travels and speeches (even though within the constraints indicated).

- Operator: NATIS' own activities: visits to HQ, publications, fellowship programmes, for example.
  The SG's travels and speeches, as above.
- Controller: NATIS controls the national organizations' implementations, as far as this is possible.

These are crucial roles that imply the exertion of much influence. To complement the picture, however, we should also mention some less influential roles that are played by the IS in information: communication facilitator, expert/coordinator, and mediator. To repeat an example of the latter role, the 'map adjustment' mentioned above between Greece and Turkey could be seen as an example of IS mediation.

It is beyond doubt that the IS manages to play some of the 'heaviest' roles in terms of influence that were stipulated in Part I. Even though only part of the information activities are carried out by NATIS itself, this is compensated for by the budget decisions regarding national organizations and also, of course, the activities of the SG. Regarding the budget decisions, it deserves to be repeated that they involve considerable adjustments from one year to the next for certain countries, not just marginal ones. And they are actually *decisions*, that is, they do not have to be approved (or even discussed) in any of the committees in the area. Hence, national influences on these decisions seem to be modest or negligible.

In relative terms, in comparison to the two other fields that have been investigated, it is obvious that the IS is most influential in information. Even in infrastructure, the strongest of the two other fields, the IS had no significant initiating role (for example, making priorities among projects), and only a controller role in the process of implementation. So even if the budget is much larger in infrastructure (a dubious comparison, one should add),[65] what we are interested in here is that the influence of the international civil servants relative to that of national civil servants is significantly more in favour of the former in information than in infrastructure.

Explaining the IS Influence in the Information Area

We shall now see if an explanation can be provided for the relatively influential position of the NATO IS in the information area. According to the general issue-area model in Figure 6 (p. 71), we should turn our attention to the 'basic character' of IO information as an issue area.

First of all, what is the 'height' of information as an issue area? National top decision-makers do not, apparently, perceive the area as vital to national core values, as the field is almost totally delegated to civil servants. Only at few occasions, it is taken up by the North Atlantic Council, and then mostly in a routine manner. Hence, it should clearly qualify as 'low politics'. Indicative of this status is also the fact that member countries have accepted the uncertainty implied by a common budget and common programmes.

Turning to the needs' location, IO information is obviously a 'within need'. The IO wishes that populations in member countries, perhaps with emphasis on selected groups, are informed about its purposes and policies. Even though this requires a certain minimum of coordination between countries there can be no doubt that the perceived need in question is located *within* countries: their respective populations.

IO information, hence, belongs to type I of basic characters of issue-areas (see Figure 7, p. 78). According to the issue-area model, ICSs in such areas should be able to get a relatively high influence *vis-à-vis* their environment, and relative to national civil servants. This seems to be in fine correspondence with our conclusion to the previous section.

We shall now go through the intermediate factors in the model that seem to have been decisive, in this particular area, for the relatively high influence exerted by the ICS. It seems that the status as low politics is the one factor carrying the strongest explanatory power. The ensuing uncertainty acceptance, first and foremost illustrated by the common budget, has led to an operative implementation responsibility to NATIS, and to the availability of budget sanctions *vis-à-vis* national organizations. As to the latter, the national organizations are likely to anticipate this sanction and, hence, let their supported activities be influenced by NATIS guidelines. Otherwise, they risk a reduction or even a denial of future programmes. This sanction applies both at the aggregate, national level (that is, nations, as a rule, wishing to become 'high priority' countries),[66] and within nations, where different associations may compete for the same piece of the cake. The fact that the IS is able to decide, by itself, the allocation of positive sanctions to clients, and to alter this allocation significantly from one year to the next, is a highly remarkable factor.

Regarding the operative implementation responsibility, we have seen that it, *eo ipso*, entails a considerable influence on which activities are being performed. This can be ascribed again to the 'low politics' status of the area: the infrequent meetings of the Information Committee, and the non-experts, often amorphously instructed, that most delegations send to it.[67] This leaves almost all initiative with the IS. This is a source of influence in itself, of course. But the operative role has probably also given NATIS officials an expertise and a routine in their tasks that the non-experts from delegations, with several other fields to cover, can hardly compete with. As regards the country activities, however, where NATIS is only a controller, one must believe that the expertise advantage belongs to the national information officials. They are the ones who can be expected to be intimately familiar with the specific national policies and perceptions, target groups, and linguistic nuances crucial to PR materials (for example, Jordan, 1967, pp. 187–188; de Sousa, 1985, p. 29, i 37). This national expertise advantage is, in the first place, the reason for the decentralized information structure.[68] But it must also, at least to a certain extent, be assumed to weaken the efficiency of the NATIS controller role.

The fact that information is a 'within need' does not seem to be as important as its 'height'. According to our theoretical thinking, information should be an insatiable need that could never be argued to be really fulfilled, and where it would always be possible to argue for an extra effort. Few needs are so flexible as 'information', whatever its specific content. However, there has been a complete standstill as regards NATIS personnel size from 1975 to 1987 (see Figure 11). Also as to budget, a 'regime of zero real growth' has been prevailing in recent years (i 37, Astori, 1987, pp. 23–6).[69]

The needs' location does, however, lead to a more favourable client/ authority constellation than in either of the two other areas. NATIS does indeed have secondary clients, some of which are quite far from government circles: certain identification actors that, to some extent, resemble grassroot movements, and individual, humble research fellows, beneficiaries of NATIS's research programmes. These secondary clients are likely to follow NATIS's guidelines carefully, in order to get the future support, they probably wish.

By and large, however, it seems that low politics is the essential explanatory factor in our area at hand. And it works stronger in information than in infrastructure: it has given the IS both an operative and a controller role in information, versus only the latter in infrastructure (though here supported by less ambiguous engineering standards, we should add). It has given NATIS a budget sanction that is absent, at least to the IS, in infrastructure. This should explain by way of the model's logic, the more influential position to the IS in information than in infrastructure. *Outside* the model's logic, infrastructure has grown in virtue of certain technological developments (see p. 101). But this is more than equalized by another exogenous factor, the vital role of the SG in information, described at some length above. The SG cannot, by far, play corresponding roles in force planning or infrastructure. The Office is, so to speak, tailored to PR activities. The three factors that were emphasized as crucial to the SG's PR abilities (political career background, personality factors, including working style, and native language) in no way belong to an issue-area model, as the one at stake here. Fulfilling our criteria for an international civil servant, the SG's influence in the area should, of course, be included in the overall assessment of the IS influence in the field. We must recognize, though, that it is a factor exogenous to the issue-area model (see further on p. 128).

Notes – Part III

1. The same goes for the EC. See Scheinman (1971, p. 193) or Michelmann's (1978, pp. 13, 231) comparison of various directorates.
2. See, for example, Lundqvist (1987, chapter 7.1). See also Mouritzen (1988), Part IV and its references, where national Foreign Ministries are regarded as 'producers' of foreign policy inertia, not intended at the top.
3. See McLaren's survey of literature (1980a, pp. 19–24).

4. The distinction corresponds, roughly, to the one between 'service organizations' and 'forum organizations', by Cox and Jacobson (1974, pp. 5–6). Both distinctions stipulate ideal types, of course: classifications of IOs (or their issue areas) according to them cannot always be made unambiguously. Cox and Jacobson (*ibid.*) also support hypothesis (1) mentioned in the text.
5. For discussions of problems connected to the concept of 'issue area', see, for example Zimmermann (1973) or Underdal (1979).
6. For some typologies of (national) values, see Mouritzen (1988, pp. 41–50).
7. One could, alternatively, choose to regard the question of common programmes as an independent factor, empirically closely related to the height of politics.
8. Which does not exclude, of course, that one could think of further 'fundamental' properties.
9. In the presentation of the model's reasonings, I shall avoid examples (except for a few very special ones).
10. Uncertainty avoidance was initially introduced at the end of Part II (pp. 60–1), being an underlying factor 'responsible' for ICSs lack of self-control. See, for instance, Cyert and March (1963, pp. 118–120), emphasizing negotiation with the environment as a means towards reducing uncertainty of firms, or Thompson (1967). As to a foreign policy context, see Allison (1971, chapter 3), or Mouritzen (1988, chapter 22, notably p. 320).
11. The argument here could also serve as an elaboration of the argument in the previous section for the absence of common programmes in connection with high politics.
12. One can wonder here, why McLaren has no hypothesis pertaining to the height of politics. It may be ascribed to the fact that the UN specialized agencies, he has investigated, are relatively homogeneous in this regard, that is, belonging to low politics.
13. Ascher (*ibid.*), in his analysis of the World Bank, sees both sides of the coin. On the one hand,

In the absence of clear-cut priorities, the signals from the organizations's leadership are more likely to be ambiguous... [this] leaves greater scope for staff discretion and greater importance in choosing from among these options... .

On the other hand,

Clear objectives and priorities may limit the staff's power within the organization but strengthen the organization with respect to its environment [that is, its secondary clients].

Whereas the argument pertaining to the secondary clients is fully consistent with my view, the argument regarding the relationship to the IO authority is not. However, as also pointed out by Ascher, the World Bank is, for a number of other reasons, one of the most powerful ICSs that exist; this makes it a somewhat special case in relation to my argument above. See also the comments below on the expertise factor.

14. It is argued by Downs (1967, p. 265 and chapter VI) that

The rules governing specific functions of a bureau are more likely to be elaborate, extensive and inclusive:
a) the more repetitive or routine the actions required
b) the more predictable and stable the situations normally faced by the bureau in carrying out those functions
c) the longer the bureau has carried them out
d) the less the importance of the decisions involved... .

15. Point (c) was presupposed in our reasoning above. (a), (b) and (d) comprise, roughly, what we have labelled 'low politics'. Hence, also in a national context as such, low politics seems to favour the kind of complexity of rules that, in turn, strengthens the civil service. Which does not, of course, prevent member countries from having a long range of 'safeguard procedures' at their disposal to avoid EC rules.

    It is interesting to note here that the relevance of the Court seems to vary with issue-areas. For instance, it is more important when it comes to environmental protection than in the case of member countries' economic policies. It would require special investigations to find out if these variations are systematically connected to the height of each area.

    On the EC Court in general, see Rasmussen (1986).

16. It should be admitted here that I have not entirely understood McLaren's reasoning; what follows is, to some extent, my own interpretation and elaboration.
17. As we remember (p. 52, in particular Note 23), also the number of national civil servants (in the delegations (devoted to the area in question) is important, depending, though, on where the primary implementation responsibility lies.
18. These internal positive sanctions in the hands of the ICS leadership should not, evidently, be mistaken for the sanctions *vis-à-vis* the external world, previously dealt with.
19. The sub-division of the NATO ICS (= the IS) into directorates is almost identical to the committee structure; see Figure 11.
20. This assertion will be justified in the respective chapters below.
21. Infrastructure is an area that NATO (*Infrastructure Manual*, chapter 1, p. 1), itself is 'proud' of:

    ...this common infrastructure is one of the outstanding achievements of the Alliance.

    Jordan (1967, p. 265, also p. 286) describes infrastructure as:

    ...that aspect of the Alliance which came nearest to supranationalism.

    This judgement, of course, refers to the early years of the Alliance. But the description 'supranationality' is also used by one of my interviewees (i 5).

22. It should be stressed here, though, that the regular force goals process described below, is not synonymous with NATO's defence planning as a whole. And the IS may play a slightly more important role in the longer-term planning process than in the regular process dealt with here (i 35).
23. For a survey of NATO's institutional structure, see pp. 6–8.
24. Instructed by the Danish Ministry of Defence or Ministry of Foreign Affairs. Formally speaking, instruction should only be by the Chief-of-Staff. A certain dilemma can be imagined for MC members in matters with strong political overtones as, for example, the 'zero solution' regarding middle-range nuclear missiles that the Superpowers agreed upon in 1987. The military instruction may say that the solution is militarily unfortunate, whilst the political recommendation ('adjustment') is positive, seeing the agreement in an East–West *détente* perspective.
25. This 'confrontation procedure' (the 'close examination of the policies of each actor by other actors and by the international institution' – Taylor, 1978a, p. 199) stems originally from the OEEC/OECD, where member-countries' economic policies are confronted and sought coordinated. As to this procedure during the first years of the Alliance, see Jordan (1967, chapter X, notably p. 222). Certain countries were appointed as 'opponents' to the country in the 'hot seat'.
26. It should also be emphasized here that *vis-à-vis* third parties, the USA is the strong party in this 'community of attitudes'. At the multilaterals, a small power like, for example Denmark, will be more sensitive to American criticism of its defence effort (and German criticism, we should add) than criticism from the IS.

27. And one must agree with NATO's *Facts and Figures* (1984) that the exchange of information that is involved here about such a sensitive subject as military forces is something quite unique between countries in peacetime (or perhaps even in war). See further Note 28.
28. Taylor (1978b, p. 225) mentions an example from the interwar period: in 1922, negotiations between the two War allies, Britain and France, about the possibility of agreeing contingency plans between General Staffs to cope with any new German attack were broken off by the British on the grounds that such plans involved giving too much away to another country (that is, uncertainty avoidance).
29. For a NATO/EC comparison in this regard, see Taylor (1978a) and Taylor (1978b, pp. 221, 227).
30. One addition should be made here, though: member governments can rhetorically simulate *vis-à-vis* domestic opinion that possible sanctions from other member-countries are, in fact, sanctions from NATO institutions, that is, exploit the vagueness of the term 'NATO'. It is much easier to justify an expense by referring to a NATO decision than by referring to the wish of country X. The former hints the morally evident principle of living up to decisions in an IO (again, being a 'depository of legitimacy'); the latter will, to some extent, sound like a national humiliation. In this sense, then, NATO's common force planning can be a rhetorical asset for member governments. It can be (Taylor, 1978a, p. 204)

...a point of reference, or a pole of attraction in national defence decision-making.

31. Lord Ismay was NATO's first Secretary General, serving 1952–1957.
32. And one should remember, of course, that the evaluation of 'excuses' is also made by other member countries, even though to varying degrees (not least the USA, having the best personnel resources, also drawing upon its embassies in the relevant capitals).
33. See also Hellebust (1974, p. 5), or NATO's *Facts and Figures* (1984, p. 188) or *Infrastructure Manual* (henceforth referred to as *Manual*) (chapter 5, p. 2).
34. As expressed in *Manual* (chapter 1, p. 5):

Installations should have a degree of common use and/or common interest for nations participating in the integrated military structure of the Alliance.

35. There is a special symbolic value attached to those projects, where NATO itself functions as 'host country' (that is, host for the installations in question). This is the case for certain communications projects.
36. MNCs write 'impact statements', so that decision-makers can see the operational implications of various possible ceilings (*Manual*, chapter 2, p. 9).
37. This is an independent committee under the Council. Like the Infrastructure Committee, its Chairman is provided by the Infrastructure Directorate.
38. The IS, Infrastructure Directorate, secures that cash flows take place between member countries in accordance with the requirements of the common budget (*Manual*, chapter 4, pp. 24–25).
39. Jordan (1967, p. 281) comments the auditing procedure:

It was deemed especially important that there should be no irregularities because this was the only major NATO activity for which the nations had pooled their economic resources.

40. See, for example, Jordan (1967, p. 271) for an example:

The fourth slice, set a £297 000 000 in the first place, was reduced by the Supreme Commanders to £182 000 000 by retaining only those items which they foresaw would be needed by 1954. The Council further reduced this figure to £80 000 000 by directing the military planners to defer... estimates for all projects which did not need to be started immediately.

41. IAU = 'Infrastructure Accounting Unit'. 1 IAU = £1.00 prior to the 1967 devaluation (NATO, *Facts and Figures*, 1984, p. 189).
42. As formulated by a delegation infrastructure expert (i 16):

    And we had an enormous quarrel that lasted for almost 2 years, in order to find a ceiling for the present slice group. From the military side, they wanted a ceiling of almost 6 billion IAU, that is, the double of what we eventually got. But there was simply no political backing for such a large increase.

    It deserves to be added here that *national* military authorities are not normally enthusiastic about high ceilings. This is so, because the infrastructure contributions to the common funding are taken out of national military budgets (i 38).
43. It should be mentioned, though, that a revision was decided in 1979 for Turkey and Portugal, with reference to the economic situation of these countries (NATO, *Facts and Figures*, 1984, p. 190).
44. As should appear, we are here dealing with another type of 'cost sharing' than the one described in the previous section. Here, we refer to specific projects, whose financing is shared between the host country and NATO's common budget (see *Manual*, chapter 4, p. 2).
45. 'The elaboration only, the technical side' (i 5). A more detailed elaboration is made in connection with the screening of countries' applications to the Payments and Progress Committee, that is, after the formal slice approval in the DPC (see *Manual*, chapter 7, pp. 3, 10).
46. Meaning that one has, in advance, decided which company shall be contracted.
47. It was actually considered during the first years of the Alliance to station technicians permanently in individual member countries (Jordan, 1967, p. 278). The idea was, however, abandoned, among other things in order to emphasize the national authorities' responsibility for the construction of installations.
48. It is emphasized (i 38), though, that member governments are eager to ask questions pertaining to their respective installations:

    It is easy enough to ask questions; the burden of proof actually lies with the host country.

49. We should also remember from the above analysis that the controller role could be coupled to a mediating role, in cases where countries other than the one directly involved chose to engage themselves.
50. In addition to these four assessments, there is one deviant conception (i 8). The interview person in question though, had no personal experience with infrastructure. It can be inferred from these statements, in my view, that the IS is relatively strong in infrastructure (and stronger than in force planning); not that it is necessarily *the* strongest field. Looking at Figure 11 (as the interviewees did at the occasion), it is too much to claim that they, at short notice, should be able to survey all kinds of 'odd' fields covered by NATO.
51. Such as Denmark's freezing of its contribution to installations pertaining to the middle-range nuclear missiles (INF).
52. And correspondingly inside the IS: the Secretary-General is, occasionally, engaged in matters pertaining to cost sharing (and perhaps ceiling); normally, the Infrastructure Directorate works entirely on its own. Van Lynden (1974, pp. 26, 29) complains about politicians' relative indifference to infrastructure (he was 'deputy controller' in the Directorate). This tendency could be found already during the first years of the Alliance (Jordan, 1967, pp. 279, 285).

120 The International Civil Service

53. And we should also remember here that there exists *national* infrastructure outside the framework of NATO infrastructure.
54. It can be mentioned, for instance, that communications projects got less than 5 per cent of the budget in the beginning of the 1950s: in 1990, it gets over 30 per cent (i 16).
55. Also, reductions in the US troops in Europe that seem likely at the present moment (1989–1990) will generate needs for better facilities for the reception of reinforcement forces (i 38).
56. This is another way of saying that the controller role during implementation also affects the factor of growth (in personnel), see Figure 6. Apart from the four engineering sections, the directorate also has a 'Budget and Analysis Section' (*Manual*, chapter 1, pp. 27–29). This section serves as secretariat for the IPPC.
57. ...the nations would hardly send a fool, because the field is so important. (i 14)

    As was mentioned in Part II (pp. 41–4), the quota system of recruitment leads to certain remarkable exceptions to this (also i 10, i 38). Furthermore, the lack of a career service leads to recruitment problems regarding the engineers that seek employment on their own initiative.
58. For instance, there has been no NATO response (at least of this type) to the Danish freezing mentioned in Note 51.
59. On this type of 'micro-management' in the early years of the Alliance, see Jordan, 1967, pp. 190–191. Jordan describes the origin of the book *NATO – The First Five Years 1949–54*, a kind of early *Facts and Figures*. Even though a carefully written factual account, it had to be an 'agreed text' between delegations. And not only delegations:

    Every Division or function of the International Staff/Secretariat discussed in the book wanted sympathetic treatment and the same amount of space.

60. To be slightly source critical here, one could mention that the committee member in question has specialized in the information field during his career. Sitting in a committee on an equal footing with younger diplomats (covering several fields), hence, may be 'responsible' for the frustration that appears from some of his comments.
61. With the addition that decentralization should not be an excuse, as it is for certain countries, just to lean back and do very little (i 37). As expressed diplomatically in a NAA report (Clark, 1986, p. 39):

    The fact that information on NATO is primarily a national responsibility should be taken to mean that member governments should be as active as possible. This principle should not be taken as an excuse for preventing NATO from acting from Brussels without the public being informed from individual capitals.

62. With the difference, though, that the roles as 'active bridge-builder' and 'initiator' have been *formally* ascribed to the SG by the North Atlantic Council, through its approval of the 'Report of the Committee of Three' in 1956 (§§ 57, 102) (in different terminology, of course).
63. And it also, evidently, enhances his authority in the Council (among his former colleagues, often).
64. As a curiosity, it is interesting to note (Jordan, 1967, p. 176, note 10) a similar opposition in the mid-1950s from the ASG for Political Affairs to the same arrangement.
65. As building high-technology installations costs more than printing information booklets (for example), budget comparisons do not seem to be very meaningful. (Growth figures for one and the same directorate can be meaningful, and the same goes for comparisons of personnel size between directorates.)

The Influence of the International Civil Service: Where, How and Why? 121

66. The sanction is somewhat modified, though, by certain impartial considerations of necessity (as with infrastructure installations). In other words, if an information need is said to exist, it is not reduced by bad management of funds; quite the contrary.
67. On this problem for small state delegations at a more general level, see Jacobson, 1984, pp. 101–103. Typically, small state delegates have less precise instructions than other delegates. In low politics, they may sometimes have to manage without instructions whatsoever, one could add (i 35).
68. By reading NAA reports on the national information activities (for example, Skaarstein, 1988; van Weezel, 1989), one gets a vivid impression of the national heterogeneities prevailing – heterogeneities that clearly seem to justify the existing decentralized structure.
69. For instance, no extra appropriations were granted for 1989, the year of NATO's 40'tieth anniversary. Expenditures for the extra information activities at this occasion had to be taken out of the existing budget (i 37).

Part IV Conclusions, Methodology and Method

Conclusions

In order to avoid unnecessary repetition, we shall draw together our conclusions of Part III here in connection with the book's general conclusions.

This work has sought to establish the foundation for general theory pertaining to the conditions, creativity and influence of international civil services (ICSs). This foundation consists of models and singular propositions. ICSs are the bureaucracies of international organizations (IOs). As they are stipulated here, their civil servants are employed by and paid by the IO in question. This stipulation was decided, in order to single out so-called 'para-organizations', being mere aggregates of nationally stationed civil servants. This should safeguard our focus as reasonably coherent units, with a certain minimum of self-control (though not impressive, see below).

There is not much point in a theoretical effort, if its focus is not a phenomenon in its own right. It is argued that the ICS is, indeed, worthy of its own independent consideration. It has four or five peculiarities *vis-à-vis* national administrations that all, ultimately, can be traced from its location in a milieu consisting of the world's most powerful actors, that is, nation states. The most significant of these is argued to be its somewhat questionable degree of self-control. Although controlling its subunits is a problem for all allegedly hierarchical systems, it is argued to be particularly acute in the type of surroundings that the ICS finds itself. The IO member states (their bureaucracies) will try to control 'their' fellow countrymen in the ICS, as far as possible. How the ICS copes, and could cope, with this problem is the sole subject of Part II.

The problem is argued to be crucial, because self-control is related to the factor of ICS creativity and, hence, influence capability (see Figure 3, p. 39). The factors that are ultimately 'responsible' for the very problem are seen as parameters; the model, we establish, encompass those factors with an effect on self-control and influence capability that can be the subject of conscious manipulation. In other words, the analysis is prescriptive: which factors should be changed in what direction, *if* the ICS, or its IO member countries, wish to improve its self-control and influence capability? According to the conception here construed, the 'counterweight' conception, a range of factors are important (as shown in Figure 3), but the two most crucial ones are the existence of a career service for the international civil servants and their recruitment on the basis of merit (versus national quotas). The counterweight conception is discussed in relation to some other schools of thought in the self-control question: the 'classical' conception (advocated, primarily, by former Secretary-Generals), the resignist conception (often argued by civil servants, national and international alike), and finally the 'utopian' school. The general model of the counterweight school is applied to a NATO ICS context, and it is argued here that a slightly modified version of the counterweight model would be the most suitable basis for a reform. It is not believed however, that such a reform is very likely, as the NATO member countries, on a par with other IO members, do not *want* creative and influential ICSs, as part of their general uncertainty avoidance (see further Note 6).

Part I stipulates the values, goals and roles of the ICS, on the basis of, notably, the ICS external relationships. A crucial factor for the general ICS position as regards autonomy and influence-capability is what can be labelled the 'client–authority constellation' in its environment. The more diversification of ICS dependence, the more favourable its position. In other words, the more clients, and notably *types* of clients, and the more sources of budget funding, the better the position of the ICS is likely to be. Or to put it the other way round – if clients and authority are identical (= 'primary clients'), and the *only* type of client, then the ICS will be in a weak position indeed.

But when it comes to the authority of the ICS and its constituent authority actors (= member countries), the opposite view is argued at some length. ICSs are so weak actors in relation to IO member countries that they will only get the disadvantages, not the conceivable advantages of 'tension between the strong'. For this and other reasons, harmony between the IO member countries can be regarded as a goal for the ICS. Moreover, it can be argued that the ICS itself is particularly qualified as a 'harmonizer', that is, playing the various bridge-building roles that were stipulated: communication facilitator, passive and active mediator, and conflict preventor.

A range of environmental factors were argued to be crucial for the very *need* of bridge-building (as formulated in the four propositions p. 24): the more heterogeneity and level of conflict between IO member countries, the less implementation responsibility to the ICS versus that of member countries, the stricter the IO decision-rules, and the more pluralism in member countries' political system, the more urgent the need for bridge-building between IO member-countries (by the ICS, not least).

NATO is classified according to our reasoning on client–authority constellations and the need for bridge-building. It is seen, at this general level, as having a rather unfavourable client–authority constellation (to be modified below), and a need of bridge-building that approaches the maximum that one can logically imagine. On the basis of this crude classification, we can expect that there is an urgent need for NATO ICS bridge-building, but also that the influence capability to carry it out may be questionable.

The Issue-Area Model

Turning to Part III, we spring from the preconditions of the ICS, be they external or internal, to what the ICS and its civil servants are actually doing. In other words: where and how is ICS influence exerted, and why? The 'why question' is answered by starting from a theoretical model, labelled the 'issue-area model'. It asserts that fundamental properties of issue areas (constituting their 'basic characters') can explain the influence exerted by ICSs in the area in question, relative to national civil services. In other words, aggregate analyses of an ICSs influence in general terms are seen as blurring reality, and are therefore abandoned in favour of analyses of separate issue areas. The two fundamental properties of issue areas are the 'height' of the area (high politics versus low politics), and the location of the needs at stake: are they 'within needs' (within member countries) or 'between needs' (between countries)? The latter property is inspired by McLaren, who is criticized, though, for not distinguishing adequately between the needs' location and the question of common programmes for the ICS. The latter factor is seen here as an analytically independent factor that is closely connected, though, to the height of politics. Each of the two fundamental properties exert an impact of its own, through various channels, on ICS influence (see Figure 6, p. 71). Areas of 'within needs' entail more ICS influence than 'between needs'. This follows from better opportunities for growth (more elastic needs at stake), and from a stronger position *vis-à-vis* clients (for example, the existence of secondary clients). As to the second property, low politics strengthens ICS influence in virtue of a minor role played by uncertainty avoidance (than in high politics), a more favourable balance of sanctions for the ICS (budget sanctions, for example), a stronger implementation role for the ICS, and an ensuing expertise advantage (relative to national civil servants.).

The two properties entail four logical combinations ('basic characters' of issue areas), of which three are relevant to the study of ICSs. On the basis of the reasonings summarized above, we get the following expectations: in case of low politics, and 'within needs' to fulfil, we expect high influence to the ICS in the area. If only the former condition is fulfilled, we expect medium influence, and if none of the conditions is fulfilled, we expect low influence. The expectations, and hence the model, are challenged by analysing the ICS influence in areas that qualify as the three basic characters: NATO information, NATO infrastructure and NATO force planning. The influence is measured, chiefly, through an analysis of the roles played by the ICS in each area.

As regards force planning, it was found that the NATO ICS exclusively plays roles in the modest end of the influence spectrum: coordinator, communication facilitator, passive mediator and observer in the implementation process (the least influential of the three stipulated roles for this process). It is *not* an initiator of proposals. The modest influence that can actually be ascribed to the ICS is mainly due to its drafting of the so-called 'country chapters' and other written material.

In infrastructure, the ICS manages to play some more influential roles: active mediator, a strong expert and controller role (during implementation), and the identity role (in addition to some more modest ones). But still, it lacks the most influential roles like operator or initiator.

These two roles are found in information, together, with a controller role (and, again, some more modest roles). In other words, some of the 'heaviest' ICS roles are played in the information area. The rank order, in terms of influence to ICSs relative to that of national civil servants in the area, hence, is obviously the following: (1) information, (2) infrastructure, and (3) force planning.

This means that our expectations, derived from a theoretical model, fit with observations of reality. However, such fitting could be the result of exogenous factors, rather than the virtues of the model and its constituent propositions. In order to shed light on this possibility, we should focus on some of the intermediate reasonings for each of the three areas. Force planning is relatively simple, as it scores low on all intermediate factors. What, after all, provides the ICS with a modest influence here, the drafting process, is a factor exogenous to the model. This creates no problems for the model's reasonings; if anything, it throws their validity in relief – were it not for its existence, the basic character of force planning would cause its ICS to be even less influential.

When it comes to the two remaining areas, it has already been noted in the information chapter that the differences as to influence can be ascribed to the height of politics more than to the needs' location. The opposite should be expected, according to the model's reasonings: what distinguishes the two areas as to basic character is precisely the needs' location. We have also seen, for that matter, a more favourable client – authority constellation in information than in infrastructure, given the weak secondary clients in the former area. The impact of this factor, however, does not seem impressive, as far as it is possible to verify. The channel that really creates problems is the one based on McLaren's reasoning: that 'within needs' should be rather elastic or flexible and, hence, cause more ICS growth (and influence). This does not happen with information, as we saw, even if this should be a paradigm example of a flexible and insatiable need. Regarding the 'between need' of infrastructure, the development up till around 1980 corresponds to McLaren's thought, that is, the need being reasonably satiated. Then an exogenous factor, the technological development, makes the field grow, as if a 'within need' were at stake.

What makes the overall influence result 'right' in information (compared, for example, with infrastructure) is the impact from an exogenous factor, the Secretary-General's role in the field, and a stronger impact from low politics than in the case of infrastructure. The former factor, being exogenous, does not really count, as far as the model's reasonings are concerned (see below). The latter does, indeed. The reason, why low politics works stronger in information than in infrastructure may be simply that information is lower politics than infrastructure. In our classification here, we have distinguished dichotomously between 'low politics' and 'high politics', in order not to proliferate the number of 'basic characters'. However, the height of politics is, as previous emphasized, a continuous factor. And by virtue of, for example, delegations' attitudes to the two areas,[1] it seems fair to say that information is lower politics than infrastructure. This afterthought, though, is in no way inconsistent with the model's reasoning – quite the contrary, it reinforces our belief in the height of politics as a crucial explanatory factor.

Lessons for the Model?

When confronting an ideal typic model (see p. 130) like the one here at stake with relevant segments of reality, it always raises the question, whether some lessons concerning the model have been learned, and whether it should even be revised before further use. Seen from the surface, everything seemed unproblematic: the expectations derived from the model were all fulfilled.

However, having looked at the intermediate explanations, one might be tempted to revise the model in certain regards. We shall discuss these, one at a time.

The ICS preparation of meetings, etc.   The drafting of written materials that was ascribed a special importance in the case of force planning leads our attention to a more general category, subsumed under 'initiation at more modest levels' (see p. 20). It encompasses such activities as the preparation of meetings (including agenda setting, the writing of background reports, collection of 'relevant' information), the chairing of meetings, the writing of meeting reports, and the suggestion and elaboration of guidelines for the implementation process. It sounds reasonable that the activities mentioned (or some of them) generally entail influence to the ICS (Eriksen, 1967, pp. 45–46, 53–57; i 1, i 2, i 5, i 6 and i 12 (chairing only); i 11 (agenda setting only); disputed, though, as regards the preparation of meetings by McLaren, 1980a, chapter 8). However this may be, it is not really the issue here. Even if the activities should exert a systematic influence, it would probably be issue neutral, as these

128 *The International Civil Service*

activities take place in all committees of an IO, roughly speaking. Hence, they hardly belong to an issue-area model. The reason why the influence of drafting was felt in one particular directorate, is simply that this directorate (force planning) is weak on other sources of influence. Hence, it weighs heavier, relatively speaking.

The Secretary-General's contribution to information   In view of the – admittedly – strong impact of this exogenous factor, one could legitimately ask whether it could somehow be incorporated in the model. The Office of the Secretary-General is – probably in all IOs – tailored to PR activities for the IO, by virtue of its symbolic value. But some of its incumbents are more tailored to these activities than others. The following factors at the individual level were emphasized: political career background, personality factors (including working style) and native language.

It seems that the Secretary-General's roles and influence varies between issue areas, judged from the NATO experience alone. But it is hard to see if it varies much differently from the rest of the ICS and, if so, with which factor(s). In order not to ruin the model's overall simplicity (see pp. 130–1), we shall not include a special factor for the Office as such.[2] It may be lack of imagination, but it is hard to see, at least to the present author, how this should be done in an elegant fashion.

The two fundamental properties   That an exogenous factor, like technological development, disturbs the picture somewhat regarding needs' elasticity, is no problem to the model. We just learn that the elasticity can be affected by something other than needs' location. As we saw, the model seemed to work fairly well in one case and fairly poorly in another.[3] What is rather serious about the latter case is that it seems difficult, at least to the present author, to find a satisfactory *ad hoc* explanation as to *why*. This should put a question mark behind McLaren's reasoning on the elasticity of 'within needs'. It is not falsified, evidently. Given McLaren's general reasonings, his UN cases, and the one satisfactory case here, there is all reason to retain it in the model, until further experiences have been made. The analytical revision made in this book, that is, removing the question of common programmes from the need's location, may reveal that the latter factor is not very strong in itself. According to the ideal typic model, the factor should be able to stand on its own feet. We may now be allowed to put a question mark behind this belief.

An innovation in relation to McLaren's way of thinking was the introduction of the height of politics as a crucial (or *the* crucial) explanatory factor. Not only can it be argued to have an impact on ICS influence through four different channels that are analytically independent of each other; it has also fitted empirically in all three cases. Comparing infrastructure and information led to an even stronger belief in the height of politics, than the model itself expresses. So what has actually happened in the course of our empirical challenges to the model is a strengthening of the height factor and a weakening of the location factor. In other words: it is easier now to establish a rank order between them – it seems obvious that the height of politics is the decisive factor for international civil servants' influence in a given issue area.

Should Stipulations be Revised?

Apart from the model, one could also imagine a revision of the stipulation of central concepts, notably that of the ICS. In order to secure ICSs as coherent and stable unit with a reasonable degree of self-control, we required that the international civil servants get their salary from the IO in question. We believed with Downs (1967, p. 28) that civil servants (or human beings in broader terms) will be most responsive to those who decide on their position and income. This is a very operational definition, as it is easy, in each single case, to decide unambiguously, whether a civil servant is 'international' or not.

We have paid a good deal of attention to the MNCs in this book, naturally, but some might argue that they should actually be included, along with the IMS, into the concept of NATO ICS. Even though the military officers are paid from home, selected and stationed as part of their national careers, strongly affiliated with their respective national services, and apparently more 'instructed' from home than their ICS colleagues (i 5, i 21, i 23; Beer, 1969, pp. 194–195), it cannot be denied that the MNCs and IMS, at least from a superficial glance, seem to function very much like the ICS.

It might be interesting to ask if our results pertaining to the issue-area model would have been different with a broader ICS conception, as outlined here. Roughly speaking, it seems that we would have observed a stronger ICS influence in all three areas. The MNC military expertise would be a factor to take into account as regards force planning, but it would never be able to compensate for the low scoring on the rest of the factors in the model. As regards infrastructure, there would be a certain budget sanction regarding the allocation of future projects to countries. But as was pointed out in the chapter, considerations of military necessity behind the project allocations to countries would to a large extent undermine the credibility of this sanction. In the information field, SACEUR, simultaneously Commander-in-Chief of the US forces in Europe, plays a symbolic role that is not far from that of the Secretary-General (also paying official visits to member countries). It seems, on the whole, that adding a further layer of 'international civil servants' to those in our analysis would add influence to NATO in all three fields. But their mutual rank order, which is the essential point as far as the model is concerned, would be the same. So from the model's point of view, our results would be identical, as it seems.

As to future studies, it could also be argued that a more liberal definition of the ICS would open the gates too much for all kinds of para-organizations, where the international employments would be formal only. Should such be the objects of inquiry, it is the present author's view that they should be studied as epi-phenomena to the respective national civil services, from where the civil servants' salary and career opportunities emanate. In the words of Aristotle, it is believed that we should 'divide reality in its proper parts'. Conglomerates are not 'proper parts'; they are not phenomena in their own right that can justify an independent theoretical effort.

On the whole, therefore, it seems that the stipulation of ICSs that has been made in the present study has been justified.

Methodology and Perspectives

Methodological reflection should primarily be *post hoc*, that is, reflection on the logic of a theoretical construct that already exists (argued in Mouritzen, 1981). Long *a priori* statements of academic school affiliations are here seen as redundant, at best (see Rochester, 1986, pp. 778, 802–803 on what he labels 'fads' in IO studies).[4] Reflections on school affiliations may, if *post hoc*, be ascribed a certain pedagogical value (though entailing the risk of labelling scholars and books); but in order to be constructive, we should start out from the immanent properties of an existing theoretical construct, in order to see specifically in which directions it points as to conceivable future studies.

As described at some length in Mouritzen (1988, chapter 33), the present author's theory of knowledge is non-inductivist. Research should start out from ideal typic constructs,[5] whose primary purpose is to provide a relatively simple (some would say 'simplistic', probably) starting point for inquiry into the 'world of chaotic variety'. Somehow or other, the ideal typic construct (the 'model') must make contact with this chaos. This happens through the 'challenges'. A challenge, hence, is an operation, where expectations derived from the model are confronted with empirical observations, pertaining to the relevant segment of reality. In case of deviations between expectations and observations, they are accounted for, if possible, by pointing to 'disturbing' factors outside the model (exogenous factors).

There is no particular fear of deviations in such a setting; the model serves as a standard of normality that can also shed some light on the 'abnormalities' that one encounters. Of course, if the deviations comprise a systematic pattern, one must begin thinking of revising the model. Ultimately, we might be led to substitute it for another one, but at first, we should consider including the disturbing factors in a systematic fashion into the model. This, however, has the cost of reducing the model's original simplicity. One must always, therefore, weigh this reduction against the model's improved explanatory power.

The issue-area model and the 'lessons' to it that have been learned in the previous chapter should be an example of such a challenge procedure. As we remember, the disturbing factors were not able to inspire supplements to the model, and the question marks to one of its central propositions were not enough to think of revising it. Instead of reducing the model's simplicity, we actually came to increase it, by being able to prioritize the two 'basic properties' better than before. It should now be possible to rank order the 'height of politics' as *the* fundamental explanatory factor for ICS influence in an area.

If a good model, or theory, is one that can explain 'much by little' (simplicity!), then this model is a good one. Many things can be reasonably accounted for by pointing, mainly, to one factor. Turning to the model of ICS self-control in Part II (Figure 3, p. 39), we face a model that can explain relatively 'little by much' (even though we should remember that two of the explanatory factors were prioritized). This is a model that has not gone through the challenge procedure described above. As with the rest of the models, we have formulated the model and its constituent propositions on the basis of '*a priori* reasoning', being a rather impenetrable mixture of analytical thinking, existing theories, and unsystematic empirical knowledge that one may have of various IOs and their ICSs, and so on. The model was argued to be superior to some competing conceptions of ICS self-control. Its constituent categories were *illustrated* from a NATO ICS context. Most important, however, the model served as the basis for prescription of reform for the NATO ICS. The model was designed for this purpose, the explanatory factors being only such that, in principle, could be the subject of conscious manipulation.

The three main reasonings of Part I, that on the ICS Values, Goals and Roles (Figure 2, p. 13), the one on the client–authority constellation, and the one on the need for an ICS bridge-building effort are all, roughly speaking, at the same stage of development as the self-control model (though with no prescriptive uses). The two latter were *applied* to NATO (not challenged!), the former to a range of non-NATO examples, in order to facilitate future broader applications and challenges.

It was crucial, for its subsequent use in the analysis of influence in Part III in the issue-area model, to establish a typology of ICS roles. Like various other such typologies (that are usually more elaborate), it does not pretend to be exhaustive. Its accomplishment should be, relative to the existing typologies, that it relates the roles systematically to ICS goals and values, through assumed relations of instrumentality (means–ends relations). These basic values, in particular the political values, have been established with inspiration from values that are normally ascribed to much more powerful actors than ICSs. This, however, should link the study of ICSs closer to political science than is normally the case.

We can sum up the operations that have been carried out in relation to the various theoretical constructs presented in this book:

Part I: The three main reasonings that were mentioned:
- *a priori* reasoning
- formulation of propositions (or model)
- illustrations (outside NATO)

132 *The International Civil Service*

Part II: The self-control model:
- *a priori* reasoning
- formulation of propositions and model
- illustrations (NATO)
- the prescription of reform (NATO)

Part III: The issue-area model:
- *a priori* reasoning
- formulation of propositions and model
- *empirical challenge and lessons*

Suggestions for Further Research

On the basis of this mapping of our analytical operations, it is possible to indicate which types of further research would be desirable, given the respective models' properties and stages of development. The issue-area model, being the most developed one, can provide the most precise suggestions. If we accept that the height of politics is the decisive factor, we should expect, within a NATO context, the 'Division of Scientific Affairs', with its extra 'low politics' character, to be the one where the international civil servants would be the most influential, relative to their national colleagues. Outside a NATO context, one should study international civil servants' influence in issue areas, preferably within one and the same international organization, that represent high and low politics, respectively.

The rest of the models (reasonings), none of which distinguishes between issue areas, obviously need challenges outside a NATO context. For instance, the higher degree of career service prevailing in the EC (and to some extent the UN) would make their civil services fruitful challenges to the self-control model: are individual civil servants' dependency homewards less of a problem here than in NATO, as the model would predict? An EC challenge would be a particularly good idea, because so many exogenous factors are identical to those of NATO and, hence, can be regarded as constant. The very best challenge to the self-control model would be presented, of course, if its reform proposals were implemented (which is, however, a rather unlikely possibility, as we noted).

Further studies, like those suggested here, could contribute to remedying the lack of literature on international civil services that was pointed out in the Introduction. There are, basically, three reasons to study international civil services:

1. Their microcosmos gives an impression of the nature of the present international system.
2. They exert influence.
3. To be able to prescribe reform for them.

International civil services should *not* be the objects of inquiry on the basis of a belief that they encompass the locus of world power. In few arenas will one get such a vivid impression of the predominance of nation states in the present international system, as in the microcosmoses of international civil services. Nation states (their civil services) will try to exert an influence on everything they can manage to, often in directions that can be argued to be contrary to their own substantial interests. Uncertainty avoidance, the fear to lose control, is often more important than substance.[6]

Still, international civil services *do* exert an influence of their own. *Even* in the issue-area with the most unfavourable preconditions for influence, NATO force planning, we could observe an unambiguous influence by the international civil servants (though modest, of course). So the lack of literature that was noted initially, a lack that is particularly pronounced when it comes to the field of military security, cannot be dismissed by saying that 'they do not exert an influence of their own'. They obviously *do*, even where the odds are the most unfavourable that one can logically imagine.

One's third motivation for the study of international civil services could be of a normative nature. Even if their influences are, after all, relatively modest at present, this could be changed in the future, if developments in international politics provide increased freedom of manoeuvre for international organizations (as the trend seems to be at present (1990)). To sustain such a development, one might wish international civil services to function more creatively than at present, being the subject of frequent criticism (see the Introduction). Such a normative interest in strengthened and more creative international institutions would require prescriptive models, designed towards reforming international civil services.

Appendix on Method

The categories in our models require various research techniques, in order to be adequately observed. Many of the categories do not ask for much precision or effort to be registered, in particular those pertaining to the ICS environment. For instance, our general background knowledge permits us to state that NATO is a more homogeneous IO than the UN, regarding member countries and their types of societies. Or that the political systems of NATO countries are pluralistic seen in a global-comparative perspective.

When it comes to categories at the micro-level, regarding the contemporary decision-making processes in the closed worlds of IOs and their ICSs, we are in a difficult position indeed.[7] We must primarily rely on interviews with civil servants involved in the processes, or in a position to observe them. To this can be added memoirs by former international civil servants, typically. Below it will be described how the interviews relevant to the present study have been carried out, and the problems encountered in this connection. What will be said on the interpretation of interviews pertains also, of course, to the use of memoire literature.

In total 43 oral interviews were carried out. The two main categories of interviews were those with NATO IS officials in NATO Headquarters in Brussels, and those with (national) delegation civil servants (from four delegations), also at NATO HQ. To these categories should be added some interviews, for example, in SHAPE (in Mons, Belgium) and in the Danish Foreign Ministry (in Copenhagen). Questions were sent to the interviewees in advance, in the hope that there would be time to reflect upon them, but not with the intention of getting any written responses. The questions provided a certain structure to the, often very informal, conversations. It turned out, frequently, that spontaneous 'stories' or other comments, not specifically asked for, were the most interesting results from an interview. The interviews were written down, as soon as possible after the end of the conversation, and are included in a special report. As the interviewees, naturally, have been promised anonymity, this report is not publicly available.

As could be expected, the openness and interest of individual interviewees varied a great deal, but I benefited from the opportunity of returning to some of those where it appeared the most rewarding. A quite typical attitude was expressed by one interviewee (i 14):

> I do not at all feel uncomfortable about these questions, as they pertain to structure and function rather than policy content.

Turning to the interpretation of interviews, it should be mentioned that certain, relatively factual answers were exempt from interpretation (but not from independent checking, of course). Interpretations were made in the light of the interviewee's career background, and the institutional interests that he/she were assumed to serve. (This was taken into account also by posing different sets of questions to IS officials and to delegation civil servants.) Statements of the type 'we are better qualified here in this office, than over there' or 'we suffer from a tremendous work-load' were not regarded as interesting, but belong to normal bureaucratic rhetoric (the opposite statements, of course, would have been extremely interesting!). Statements from the various interviews were then lumped together, according to which category they pertained to. An overall judgement on the relevant category was then made, by aggregating the individual statements. In case of deviant statements, extra checks were made, or the statements were weighed according to the interviewee's career background, notably (for example, number of years within the field). In case of significant deviant conceptions, they have been stated in the text (or in the Notes section). The most corroborated conceptions are those that have been stated in more than one office, for example in the relevant directorate, a neighbouring directorate, and one or more delegations.

Conclusions, Methodology and Method 135

In certain cases, individual interview formulations have been cited, in order to convey an impression of important nuances.

It is beyond doubt that interviewing is an extremely difficult method of empirical observation, with several pitfalls when it comes to interpretation. The method has not been selected out of any positive impulse, but rather due to a lack of alternatives, when one wishes to study contemporary closed bureaucracies and their decision-making processes.

Notes – Part IV

1. See for example p. 104 (infrastructure), and pp. 107, 108 and 114 (information).
2. We have seen, at several points in this book, important roles played by Secretary-Generals. However, the analysis has always been integrated with that of the ICS as such, the SG being its prime representative. (An exception is the analysis of staff leadership, pp. 48–50, though.)
3. We did not analyse force planning in this regard, partly to avoid explanatory overkill, partly because there is no common budget in the area (theoretically, we could have used the number of employees as the sole measure of growth).
4. Rochester emphasizes (1986, p. 778), a bit polemically, the 'herd instinct' in the scholarly community, that is, that

   ...scholars may flit from one island of theory to another (for example, from regional integration to interdependence to regime formation) in keeping with the latest 'fads' that ultimately prove short-lived.

   A priori 'school discussions' exacerbate this tendency, in my view.
5. As to the notion of ideal types, see Weber (1966, pp. 17–18).
6. We should remember that governments' uncertainty avoidance is a crucial factor *both* in the self-control discussion (one of the parameters 'responsible' for the problem of ICS self-control), *and* in the issue-area model.
7. Hoggart, former ASG in UNESCO, notes in the Preface to his memoirs (1978):

   One of its [UNESCO's] great weaknesses is over-defensiveness, unwillingness to listen to criticism... The lesson – of the value of open, critical comment – is one UNESCO really must at last learn, or it will become even more of an enclosed Byzantine system than it is at present... It must learn to live less self-protectively, more bravely.'

   See also the Introduction to Pitt and Weiss (1986, p. xii), pertaining to a UN context generally. Indicative of such over-defensiveness is, for instance, limited access even to unclassified documents.

Bibliography

Allison, G.T. (1971), *Essence of Decision, Explaining the Cuban Missile Crisis*, Boston.
Ascher, W. (1983), 'New Development Approaches and the Adaptability of International Agencies: the Case of the World Bank', *International Organization* 1983:3.
Astori, G. (1987), *General Report on the Atlantic Alliance and Public Opinion*, NAA Report, Bruxelles.
Beer, F.A. (1969), *Integration and Disintegration in NATO: Processes of Alliance Cohesion and Prospects for Atlantic Community*, Columbus, Ohio.
Beer, F.A. (ed.) (1970), *Alliances: Latent War Communities in the Contemporary World*, New York.
Beer, F.A. (1971), 'Political–Military Regionalism and International Administration', in Jordan (ed.), *ibid*.
Bennett, A.L. (1988), *International Organizations. Principles and Issues*, Englewood Cliffs, New Jersey.
Birrenbach, K. (1962), 'The Reorganization of NATO', *Orbis* 1962:2.
Blumenthal, W.M. (1988), 'The World Economy and Technological Change', *Foreign Affairs* 1988:3.
Bryde, B.O. (1988), 'International PGOs?', in Hood and Schuppert (eds.), *ibid*.
Buteux, P. (1983), *The Politics of Nuclear Consultation in NATO 1965–1980*, New York.
Carrington, Lord (1984), *NATO: Politics and Defense*, speech held in New York City, 22 October, 1984.

Carrington, Lord (1986), *European Security*, speech held in Copenhagen, 5 May, 1986.
Carrington, Lord (1988), *Reflect on Things Past. The Memoirs of Lord Carrington*, London.
Clark, D. (1986), *General Report on NATO's Public Relations Problems*, NAA Report, Bruxelles.
Claude, I. (1964), *Swords into Plowshares*, New York.
Cox, R.W. (1969a), 'Introduction: Perspectives and Problems', in Cox (ed.), *ibid*.
Cox, R.W. (ed.) (1969b), *International Organizations in World Politics*, London.
Cox, R.W. (1973), 'The Executive Head: An Essay on Leadership in International Organizations' in Goodrich and Kay (eds), *ibid*.
Cox, R.W. and Jacobson, H.K. (eds) (1974), *The Anatomy of Influence*, Yale.
Crane, B.B. and Finkle, J.L. (1981), 'Organizational Impediments to Development Assistance: The World Bank's Population Program', *World Politics* 1981:3.
Cyert, R. and March, J. (1963), *A Behavioral Theory of the Firm*. Englewood Cliffs, New Jersey.
Damsgaard, A.C. (1983), *Staffing an International Civil Service: Principles and Practices*, Copenhagen.
de Cuellar, J.P. (1988), 'The Role of the United Nations in World Affairs', *International Affairs (Moscow)* 1988:10.
de Sousa, F. (1985), *Final Report of the Sub-committee on the Successor Generation*, NAA Report, Bruxelles.
Dixon, W.J. (1981), 'The Emerging Image of UN Politics', *World Politics* 1981:3.
Downs, A. (1967), *Inside Bureaucracy*, Little Brown.
Dubin, M.D. (1983), 'Transgovernmental Processes in the League of Nations', *International Organization* 1983:3.
Eriksen, B. (1967), *The Committee System of the NATO Council*, Oslo.
Flynn, G. (ed.) (1985), *NATO's Northern Allies. The National Security Policies of Belgium, Denmark, the Netherlands, and Norway*, London.
Galtung, J. (1986), 'On the Anthropology of the United Nations System', in Pitt and Weiss (eds), *ibid*.
Genton, J. (1988), *General Report on NATO and Public Opinion*, NAA Report, Bruxelles.
Ghebali, V.Y. (1986), 'The Politicization of UN Specialized Agencies: The UNESCO Syndrome', in Pitt and Weiss (eds), *ibid*.
Goldmann, K. (1979), 'Tension Between the Strong, and the Power of the Weak: Is the Relation Positive or Negative?' in Goldmann and Sjöstedt (eds), *ibid*.
Goldmann, K. and Sjöstedt, G. (eds) (1979), *Power, Capabilities, Interdependence*, London.

Goodrich, L.M. and Kay, D.A. (eds) (1973), *International Organization: Politics and Process*, Wisconsin.
Gordenker, L. & Saunders, P. R. (1978), 'Organisation Theory and International Organisation', in Taylor and Groom (eds), *ibid.*
Gould, D.J. and Kelman, H.C. (1970), 'Horizons of Research on the International Civil Service', *Public Administration Review* 1970:3.
Haas, E. (1964), *Beyond the Nation-State: Functionalism and International Organization*, Stanford.
Hammarskjöld, D. (1971), 'The International Civil Servant in Law and in Fact', in Jordan (ed.), *ibid.*
Hansen, P. (1975), *International Organisation*, Copenhagen.
Harari, D. and Bouza, J.G. (1986), 'Permanence and Innovation in International Organizations', in Pitt and Weiss (eds.), *ibid.*
Hartley, L. (1963), 'An Atlantic Commission', *Orbis* 1963:2.
Hellebust, A. (1974), *NATO Fellesfinansiert og Bilateral Infrastrukturbygging i Norge*, Oslo.
Hilf, M. (1988), 'PGOs in the European Community', in Hood and Schuppert (eds), *ibid.*
Hill, R. (1978), *Political Consultation in NATO*, Toronto.
Hofmann, W. (1987), 'Whence the Threat? The Successor Generation and the Equidistance Syndrome', *NATO Review* 1987:3.
Hoggart, R. (1978), *An Idea and its Servants. UNESCO from Within*, Oxford.
Hodd, C. and Schuppert, G.F. (eds) (1988), *Delivering Public Services in Western Europe. Sharing Western European Experience of Para-Government Organization*, London.
Ismay, Lord (1954), *NATO. The First Five Years 1949–1954*, NATO.
Jacobson, H.K. (1984), *Networks of Interdependence*, New York.
James, A. (1976), 'International Institutions: Independent Actors?', Ch. 3 in Schlaim, *ibid.*
James, R.R. (1971), 'The Evolving Concept of the International Civil Service', in Jordan (ed.), *ibid.*
Jonah, J. (1988), 'The United Nations has its Problems', *International Affairs (Moscow)* 1988:11.
Jönsson, C. (1986), 'Interorganization Theory and International Organization', *International Organization* 1986:1.
Jordan, R.S. (1967), *The NATO International Staff/Secretariat 1952–1957. A Study in International Administration*, London.
Jordan, R.S. (ed.) (1971a), *International Administration. Its Evolution and Contemporary Applications*, London.
Jordan, R.S. (1971b), 'The Influence of the British Secretariat Tradition on the Formation of the League of Nations', in Jordan (ed.) *ibid.*
Jordan, R.S. (1979), *Political Leadership in NATO: A Study in Multinational Diplomacy*, Boulder, Colorado.

Jordan, R.S. (1981), 'What Happened to our International Civil Service?', *Public Administration Review* 1981:2.
Keohane, R.O. and Nye, J.S. (1974), 'Transgovernmental Relations and International Organizations', *World Politics* 1974:1.
Larsen, B. (1986), *Fra Hierarki til Netværk*, Copenhagen.
Lewis, D. and Wallace, H. (eds) (1984), *Politics into Practice. National and International Case Studies in Implementation*, London.
Lindell, U. (1987), 'The Consensus Rule in Two International Conferences', *Cooperation and Conflict* 1987:2.
Lindgren, K. and Angell, V. (eds.) (1989), *Globalt Samarbeid: Krise eller Renessanse?*, Stockholm.
Loveday, A. (1956), *Reflections on International Administration*, London.
Lundqvist, L. (1987), *Implementation Steering. An Actor–Structure Approach*, Lund.
Mailick, S. (1970), A Symposium: Towards an International Civil Service, *Public Administration Review* 1970:3.
Manual = *NATO Infrastructure Manual* (1985), NATO.
March, J. (1965), *Handbook of Organizations*, Chicago.
Mathur, H.M. (1986), 'Experts of the United Nations in Third World Development: A View from Asia', in Pitt and Weiss (eds.), *ibid*.
McGowan, P. and Shapiro, H. (1973), *The Comparative Study of Foreign Policy. A Survey of Scientific Findings*, London.
McLaren, R. (1980a), *Civil Servants and Public Policy. A Comparative Study of International Secretariats*, Waterloo, Ontario.
McLaren, R. (1980b), 'The UN System and its Quixotic Quest for Coordination', *International Organization* 1980:1.
Meltzer, R.I. (1978), Restructuring the United Nations System: Institutional Reform Efforts in the Context of North–South Relations', *International Organization* 1978:4.
Michelmann, H.J. (1978), *Organizational Effectiveness in a Multi-national Bureaucracy*, Westmead.
Mintzberg, H. (1983), *Power in and Around Organizations*, Englewood Cliffs, New Jersey.
Modelski, G. (1970), 'SEATO', in Beer (ed.), *ibid*.
Morawiecki, W. (1968), 'Institutional and Political Conditions of Participation of Socialist States in International Organizations: A Polish View', *International Organization* 1968:2.
Mouritzen, H. (1981), 'Reflections on Self-Reflection: In Favour of a Forward-Oriented Self-Reflection in Political Science', *Statsvetenskaplig Tidsskrift* 1981:2.
Mouritzen, H. (1988), *Finlandization. Towards a General Theory of Adaptive Politics*, Aldershot.

Mouritzen, H. (1990), 'Tension Between the Strong, and the Strategies of the Weak. With Some Observations of Sweden on the Stage and Finland on the Balcony.' *Journal of Peace Research*, 1990 (forthcoming).

Myers, K. (ed.) (1980), *NATO. The Next Thirty Years. The Changing Political, Economic and Military Setting*, London.

NATO, *Facts and Figures* (1984).

Olson, Jr. and Zeckhauser, R. (1970), 'An Economic Theory of Alliances', in Beer (ed.), *ibid*.

Ørvik, N. (ed.) (1986), *Semialignment and Western Security*, London.

Pfaltzgraff, R.L. and Ra'anan, U. (eds) (1984), *National Security Policy. The Decision-Making Process*. Medford, Massachusetts.

Pitt, D. (1986), 'Power in the UN Superbureaucracy: A Modern Byzantium?', in Pitt and Weiss (eds.), *ibid*.

Pitt, D. and Weiss, T.G. (eds) (1986a), *The Nature of United Nations Bureaucracies*, London.

Pitt, D. and Weiss, T.G. (1986b), 'Introduction', in Pitt and Weiss (eds.), *ibid*.

Ramsay, R. (1984), 'UNCTAD's Failures: The Rich get Richer', *International Organization* 1984:2.

Ranshofen-Wertheimer, E.F. (1945), *The International Secretariat*, Washington D.C.

Rasmussen, H. (1986), *On Law and Policy in the European Court of Justice*, Dordrecht.

Rasmusson, R. (1986), 'UNCTAD and its Shareholders; Dialogue for Betterment', in Pitt and Weiss (eds), *ibid*.

Renninger, J.P. (1977), 'Staffing International Organizations: The Role of the International Civil Service Commission', *Public Administration Review* 1977:4.

Report of the Committee of Three: *Non-Military Cooperation in NATO* (1956), NATO.

Reymond, H. and Mailick, S. (1986), 'The International Civil Service Revisited', *Public Administration Review* 1986:2.

Rochester, J.M. (1986), 'The Rise and Fall of International Organization as a Field of Study', *International Organization* 1986:3.

Rovine, A.W. (1970), *The First Fifty Years. The Secretary-General in World Politics 1920–1970*, Leyden.

Scheinman, L. (1971), 'Economic Regionalism and International Administration: The European Communities Experience', in Jordan (ed.), *ibid*.

Schlaim, A. (ed.) (1976), *International Organization in World Politics, Yearbook 1975*, London.

Schwartz, D. (1967), 'Decision Theories and Crisis Behavior: An Empirical Study of Nuclear Deterrence in International Political Crises', *Orbis* 1967:2.

Simai, M. (1978), 'Some Problems of International Secretariats', in Taylor and Groom (eds), *ibid*.

Skaarstein, I-L. (1988), *Interim Report of the Sub-Committee on Public Information on Defence and Security: Norway, the United States, the Federal Republic of Germany and Denmark*, NAA Report, Bruxelles.
Skogmo, B. (1989), *UNIFIL – International Peacekeeping in Lebanon 1978–1988*, London.
Sloan, S.R. (1986), *NATO's Future. Towards a New Transatlantic Bargain*, London.
Smith, R.K. (1987), 'Explaining the Non-Proliferation Regime: Anomalies for Contemporary International Relations Theory', *International Organization* 1987:2.
Stafford, R.W. (1984), 'Defense Planning in NATO: A Consensual Decision-Making Process' in Pfaltzgraff and Ra'anan (eds.), *ibid*.
Stewart, J.M. (1985), 'How NATO Force Planning Works', *Jane's Defence Weekly*, June 1985.
Stikker, D.U. (1966), *Men of Responsibility. A Memoir*, London.
Taylor, P. (1978a), 'The Idea of Coordination in International Organisation', in Taylor and Groom, *ibid*. (1978).
Taylor, P. (1978b), 'Elements of Supranationalism: The Power and Authority of International Institutions', in Taylor and Groom (eds.), *ibid*.
Taylor, P. and Groom, A.J.R. (eds) (1978), *International Organisation*, London.
Thompson, J.B. (1984), 'NATO Infrastructure at a Crossroads – a Perspective', in *NATO Review* 1984:1.
Thompson, J.D. (1967), *Organizations in Action*, New York.
Thompson, J. and Gantz, N. (1987), 'Force Planning'. Conference paper.
Törnudd, K. (1982), 'From Unanimity to Voting and Consensus: Trends and Phenomena in Joint Decision-Making by Governments', *Cooperation and Conflict* 1982:3.
Underdal, A. (1979), 'Issues Determine Politics Determine Policies', *Cooperation and Conflict* 1979:1.
van Lynden, R.W. (1974), 'NATO's Silent Service', in *NATO Review 1974*.
van Wagenen, R.W. (1971), 'Observations on the Life of an International Civil Servant', in Jordan (ed.), *ibid*.
van Weezel, H.G. (1989), *Draft Interim Report of the Sub-Committee on Public Information on Defence and Security: France, the United Kingdom and Spain*, NAA Report, Bruxelles.
Vandevanter, E. (1970), 'NATO and the OAS', in Beer (ed.), *ibid*.
Väyrynen, R. (1989), 'Multilateralt Samarbete: Hegemoni eller Konkurrens?', in Lindgren and Angell (eds), *ibid*.
Wallace, H. (1984), 'Implementation across National Boundaries', in Lewis and Wallace (eds), *ibid*.
Weber, M. (1966), *Soziologische Grundbegriffe*, Tübingen.
Weiss, T.G. (1975), *International Bureaucracy. An Analysis of the Operation of Functional and Global International Secretariats*, London.

Weiss, T.G. (1982), 'International Bureaucracy: The Myth and Reality of the International Civil Service', *International Affairs* 1982:2.

Weiss, T.G. (1986), 'International Secretariat or Servant of the G 77: A Portait of UNCTAD', in Pitt and Weiss (eds), *ibid.*

Wells, C. (1986), 'The UNESCO Secretariat 'Decolonised'? Geographical Distribution of Staff 1972–84', in Pitt and Weiss (eds), *ibid.*

Winslow, A. (1970), 'Functions of an International Secretariat', *Public Administration Review*, 1970:3.

Young, O.R. (1967), *The Intermediaries. Third Parties in International Crises*, Princeton, New Jersey.

Young, T-C (1970), 'The International Civil Service Reexamined', *Public Administration Review* 1970:3.

Zimmerman, W. (1973), 'Issue Area and Foreign-Policy Process', *American Political Science Review* 1973:4.

Index

Assistant Secretary-General (ASG), 49, 58, 112
Avenol, Joseph (Secretary-General, League of Nations), 16, 17

Balance of sanctions, 75–6, 87, 104–5, 115
bridge-building, need of, 24–9, 31, 125
Brosio, 110
budget allocations to national information activities, 107–10
budget funding, 124

Career service, 44–6, 55, 58, 59, 124
central concepts, revision of, 129–30
Classical conception of ICS, the 40, 57, 124
'client-authority constellation', the, 22–3, 76, 105, 115, 124, 125, 126
communication channels (reachability), 52, 77
Conference of National Information Officers, (CONIO), 108
Conventional Defence Improvement Effort (CDI), 80, 83
cost sharing criteria, 93

counterweight conception of ICS, the 40, 55, 58, 124
Cuban missile crisis (1962), 17

Danish Foreign Ministry, 46, 47
Defence Planning Committee (DPC), 78, 80, 81, 87, 90, 92
Defence Planning Questionnaire (DPQ), 82, 84, 88
Defence Review Committee (DRC), 80, 81, 86, 87
Denmark, the defence burden and, 87
diversification of dependence, 23–4, 76, 124

environment of the ICS, the –
   actors, the crucial, 10–11
   authority for the ICS, 10, 23–4
   clients, primary and secondary, 10, 23–4
   competitors, 11
   counter-groups, 11
   identification actors, 10–11
   national civil services, 11
   bridge-building, the need for, 24–9
   change, as source of, 9–10

internal life, vs. the, 9, 10
international organisations (IOs), types of, 24–9
esprit de corps, 50–2
European Community Commission, 19, 20, 21, 43
European Community (EC), 3, 4, 5, 9, 11, 19, 20, 21, 45, 50, 57, 75
European Court of Justice, 75
European Political Co-operation (EPC), 11

Food and Agricultural Organisation (FAO), 69
France, secession from infrastructure co-operation, 98

General Agreement on Tariffs and Trade (GATT), 11
'Gorbachev effect', the, 106

Hammarskjöld, Secretary–General, 15
harmony, 12–14, 24, 31, 124
'height of politics', *see* high vs. low politics
Hierarchical functions, 35, 48, 50
high vs. low politics, 69–75, 77–8, 86, 99, 113–14, 115, 125–7, 128–9, 131, 132

inertia, 56, 57, 59
influence (of ICS), 5, 22, 67–78, 125, 132–3
  force planning, 79–89
    decision-making process, 80–2
    explaining the influence, 86–9
    roles and influence of the IS, 82–5
  information, 105–15
    explaining the influence, 113–15
    roles and influence of the IS, 112–13
  infrastructure, 89–105
    decision-making process, 90–2
    explaining the influence, 99–105
    roles and influence of the IS, 92–9
      ceiling, 92–3
      cost sharing, 93–4
      exemption from ICB, 95–7

      inspections, 96–7
      installation's residual value, 97–8
      programming of a slice, 94–5
      resulting conclusion, 98–9
Infrastructure Committee (IC), 92
Infrastructure Payments and Progress Committee (IPPC), 92, 96
Intergovernmental Maritime Consultative Organisation (IMCO), 69
International Atomic Energy Agency (IAEA), 21
International Civil Aviation Agency (ICAO), 69
International Civil Servants
  meaning, 1, 123, 129–30
  problem of dependency, 2
  typical services of, 1
International Civil Service (ICS), the –
  as a field of study, 3, 4, 10
  characteristics of, 2–3, 35–8
  coherent unit, as, 12, 123, 129
  expertise, 74, 87–8, 103–4
  growth, 76–7, 101–2, 115
    task expansion, 11, 14, 17–18, 108
  implementation and, 2, 3, 20–1, 24, 26, 73–5, 86, 102–4, 114
  preparation of meetings etc., 20, 127–8
  reasons for studying, xiii, 3–4, 123, 132–3
  roles, 14–22, 38, 82–5, 92–9, 112–3, 126
    bridge building, 14–17
    facilitating communication, 17
    conflict prevention, 14–15
    mediation, active vs. passive, 15–17
    political, 17–19
      guarding boundaries, 17–18
      instrument, 18–19
    substantial, 19–21
      expert/co-ordination, 21
      initiator, as, 20
      IO identity support, 19–20, 105, 110–2
      IO representation *vis à vis* non-members, 21

Index 147

operator/controller/observer, as 20–1
study of, plan and purpose 1–3
values, intermediate, 12–14
  political (issue neutral), 12, 22, 23
  substantial (issue specific), 12
International Competitive Bidding (ICB), 92
International Governmental Organisations (IGO), 10
International Labour Organisation (ILO), 15, 69
International Military Staff (IMS), 88, 129
International Non-governmental Organisations (INGO), 10, 11
international organisation, meaning, 1
  secretariat/programme oriented, distinction, 68, 69
  strengthening and growing numbers of, 3, 4
International Staff (NATO) (IS), *passim*
International Telecommunication Union, 69
Internationalism
  problem, the, 35–7
    crucial or not? 37–8
    nature of, 35–7
  propositions, 41–52
    bureaucratic ideology, 50–1
    career service, existence of, 44, 45
    ICS employment, national career value of, 46
    leadership, 48–9
    merit vs. quota, 41–3
    NATO: bureaucratic ideology, 51–2
    NATO: career service, 45–6
    NATO: IS employment, national career value, 46–8
    NATO: leadership, 49
    NATO: merit vs. quota, 43–4
    reachability, generally and in NATO, 52
  staff, NATO international, 53–4
    ICS internationalism, improvement of, 54–5

NATO, could/should have done differently? 55–60
interpretation of interviews and memoirs, 133–4
issue areas
  basic characters of, 5, 69–72, 76–8, 86, 99–101, 113–14, 125
  selection of for study, reasons for, 5, 78–9
issue-area model, 68–78, 125–32

Lord Carrington, *quoted*, 43, 50, 111, 112
Lord Ismay, 43, 87, 89, 93, 110

Major NATO Commands (MNC), 80, 81, 87, 90, 92, 94, 95, 103, 104, 129
Military Committee (MC), 7, 8, 80, 81, 92
Military Officers as NATO ICSs, 129
Ministries of Defence Information Officers (MODIO), 108

needs' location, 69, 70, 76–7, 86, 99, 114, 128–9
North Atlantic Treaty Organisation (NATO)
  abandoning of quotas, *discussion*, 57–8
  arguments against a career service, *discussion*, 56, 57
  force planning, 79–89
  information, 105–15
  infrastructure, 89–105
  institutional structure, 6–8
  internationalism, problem of, 53–60
  need for NATO bridge-building, 27–9
  reasons for studying, 5–6

Organisation for Economic Co-operation and Development (OECD), 88

Peace movements, 28
pluralism, 20, 26, 27, 51
policy effect, what determines, 68

Recruitment, merit vs. quotas, 41–4, 55, 57–9

resignist conception of ICS, the 40, 55, 58, 124

Secretary–General (SG), 2, 15–7, 48–50, 52, 82–3, 93–4, 110–12, 115, 128
self control, *see* internationalism
South East Asia Treaty Organisation (SEATO), 41
Spaak, 110
Stikker, *quoted* 47–8
Suez crisis, the, 15, 16, 23
Supreme Allied Commander Europe (SACEUR), 8, 52, 80, 90, 129
Supreme HQ Allied Powers Europe (SHAPE), 8, 80, 81, 90, 92, 96, 134
Major NATO Commands, 96

theoretical constructs, summary of operations relating to, 131, 132

Uncertainty, avoidance of, 60–1, 72–3, 77, 86, 99, 114, 124, 125
United Kingdom Mobile Force (UKMF), 87
United Nations (UN), 4, 43, 45 *and passim*

United Nations Conference on Trade and Development (UNCTAD), 4, 11, 18, 19
United Nations Educational Scientific and Cultural Organisation (UNESCO), 4, 36, 42
United Nations Emergency Force (UNEF), 17, 23
United Nations peace-keeping missions, 73
United Nations specialised agencies, categories, 68
United Nations Staff Regulations, form of Oath, 36
Universal Postal Union (UPU), 69
U Thant (United Nations Secretary-General), 17
Utopian conception of the ICS, the, 40, 58–9, 124

Western European Union (WEU), 11
World Health Organisation (WHO), 18, 69
World Meteorological Organisation (WMO), 50, 69
Wörner, 18